Your Career

Richard H. Buskirk

The Herman W. Lay Chair of Marketing
Southern Methodist University

CBI Publishing Company, Inc.
51 Sleeper Street
Boston, Massachusetts 02210

Your Career

Second Edition

How to plan it,
manage it,
change it

Production Editor: Becky Handler
Text Designer: Jack Schwartz
Compositor: Commonwealth Graphics

Library of Congress Cataloging in Publication Data

Buskirk, Richard Hobart, 1927-
    Your career.

    Bibliography: p.
    1. Vocational guidance.   I. Title.
HF5381.B793   1980   650.1'4   80-15509
ISBN 0-8436-0790-4

Printed in the United States of America

Printing *(last digit):* 9 8 7 6 5 4 3 2 1

Contents

Although it was my privilege to have written a number of books, I had never been asked to write a foreword for someone else's work until the first edition of this book. I am doubly delighted to have the opportunity to write the foreword for this second edition of a book that is so successful and is the best treatise on the subject of career management I have ever read.

My primary occupation for thirty years has been employment (recruiting, selection, and placement) and, since 1970, a new responsibility that I call decruitment. Decruitment is an approach to the way organizations can plan and execute terminations and still maintain a profitable and vital business by understanding the responsibilities involved. A key part of that understanding involves effective outplacement. These responsibilities have provided me with a unique opportunity to see how little effort is expended by most people and organizations in career planning.

People fail at managing their careers for a variety of reasons which are well explained in the text of this book, but there are a number of peripheral factors I feel are most crucial.

First, substantive career counseling or guidance is lacking in our educational system. Little emphasis is given in secondary schools to options other than "going to college." More and more in this day and age that advice doesn't make as much sense for a number of reasons too complex and detailed to try to explain here. Once in college, career counseling and guidance generally continue to be marginal at best.

Second, emphasis in the selection process in many organizations is programmed to what a good friend of mine calls the "EGAD" questions (expectations, goals, ambitions, and desires), which too often lead to people

Foreword

getting a job because they know how to get it—but not necessarily how to do it. My point is that the past is the best predictor of the future and the selection process must be oriented towards what was or was not done in previous jobs, not what might be done.

Third, our society judges individuals by what they do for a living and how much they earn. This forces many people into situations leading to bitterness and frustration in their careers as they attempt to "keep up with the Joneses."

Fourth, too many people after working, ten, fifteen, or twenty years must suddenly make a career decision, but are completely unprepared because they have assumed too much is preordained for them by someone else (their employer). People seldom, if ever, ask for advice or guidance on what or how well they are doing, and many of the best-intentioned organizations seldom volunteer meaningful information in this area. So we have too many people who are only trying to remain X number of years on the payroll so they can retire. When they are terminated most people blame the organization. Many times the organization is at fault, through lack of manpower controls, which allows organizations to get too fat; lip service to training and development programs; etc. Realistically, however, the individual must assume responsibility in most instances because he/she has failed in his/her own planning. Even those who leave voluntarily seldom do it on a thoughtful, planned basis. The practicalities of the situation are often overlooked because "the grass appears to be greener," and that makes a person vulnerable to momentary emotion and frustration and leads to a bad job decision. The practicalities, then, really don't become apparent until later when the romance cools.

The four factors point up dramatically the necessity for all who contemplate working, or are working, to spend time honestly appraising who they are, what they are doing or want to do, and where they are going. People must understand that career planning has to be flexible... as with any organization's objectives, give and take is necessary. Career management then is not "finality" but it should be an approach to alleviating trauma and emotion in an individual's working career. Unfortunately, many people don't see the need for any process that assists them in job or career decisions. In addition, a lot of people don't feel they have any choice—the organization or system is going to make the decisions for them.

But regardless of how much organizations talk about it, career management is primarily the individual's problem. This is as it should be because the individual, in the final analysis, must make his or her own decisions. As a matter of fact, a real danger inherent in the subject is the tendency to lean too much on someone else's advice—one must learn to use it but still make one's own decisions. Only the individuals really know their desires, ambitions, strengths, weaknesses, and motivations, and seldom do they candidly reveal these to others.

To assume the problem of career management is other than the individual's is almost as naive as assuming that job security still exists in its traditional sense. Job security nowadays is "knowing how to do what you do well enough so that you have the flexibility to do it somewhere else." This adaptability allows the individual to have alternate plans. It eliminates panic if one is suddenly terminated and makes one less prone to postponing a needed career change.

Being a rather pragmatic person, however, I know that few individuals will follow the advice as given herein. We must hope organizations will initiate and/or improve their programs of career management (counseling and guidance) as they do other facets of their personnel programs. Also, we can hope that educational institutions will begin to pay more than lip service to career guidance and counseling. There are many encouraging signs that this is happening, and organizations in particular are recognizing that their objectives are complemented by good career planning.

Finally, if the information presented in this book is understood and adapted the right way, then more people will be alert to the necessity of good career management in creating an interesting, satisfying, and challenging work life.

Donald H. Sweet
Director of Employment
Celanese Corporation

Perhaps the term "career management" needs clarification, for it may mean different things to different people. I am concerned about all of the decisions a person makes that affect his or her ability to prosper and follow a calling that is satisfying. This book is not concerned specifically with getting a better job; rather it is concerned with one's total efforts at earning a living.

It is to be expected that in discussing any topic of this importance and complexity, much disagreement will be encountered. Experts sincerely disagree with each other about many aspects of managing a career. While I try to point out many areas of disagreement in each discussion, it is difficult to do so, for even the disagreements are diverse. The reader will no doubt disagree with many things that are said. Fine! That is as it should be. You are thinking about the problem and that is the important thing—that you recognize each difficulty and give it some rational thought. You will evolve your own philosophies over time. This book should greatly help you in this development.

In any such undertaking the reader tacitly asks, "Why should I listen to you? What are your qualifications to write about this topic?" And that, too, is as it should be. It all began in 1948 when I was a senior at Indiana University. We were required to take a one-hour course called "Personal Adjustment to Business," which was simply a course in how to get a job. In the course, the professor wandered into various aspects of career management and I became greatly interested in the subject.

When I started teaching at other universities I discovered that those schools did little to help their students in career matters; it was "push them off the dock and let's see who can swim the best." I started talking about all of the subjects in this book to each senior class. The response was overwhelming. The students wanted more informa-

Preface

tion and were really grateful for the help. As the years rolled on, these same students would drift back to talk with me when they ran into some career problems. Thus, over the years I have collected a tremendous number of case histories, some of which you will read about here. Since the publication of the first edition of this book, my repertoire of case histories has been greatly enriched by its many readers who have telephoned me to discuss their career problems. And believe me, there are some real problems out there.

As for the validity of my advice, I am personally comfortable with it, for I have had considerable feedback from those people who have sought guidance. It seems to work. No doubt there are those for whom my advice did not work out, but I have yet to hear of those cases—they are kind to the old prof.

I have long wanted to write this book because I happen to think one's career is vitally important to one's welfare. So many people fail to realize their potentialities because of tactical mistakes in managing their careers. From the very beginning when I coauthored *Management of the Sales Force* in 1959, I included a chapter on careers in the book. To my frustration, reviewers have forced me to delete much of the advice you will find here from the recent editions of that book.

In this second edition of *Your Career: How to Plan It, Manage It, Change It,* I have added two major sections. The first examines the particular problems of women who want a career. The second delves into one's personality and its effect on career decisions.

Considerable material on the career problems particular to women was added because the past few years have seen a tremendous flow of women into careers. While most of the material in this book is equally applicable to both men and women, there are some career problems that women encounter that deserve special attention.

The additional material on personality factors was included because I have become more and more impressed with their importance in successful career management.

I am grateful to my assistant Marsha Kolar, who does all the hard work. I would be lost without her. She does her best to keep me out of trouble.

Your Career

PART 1

Planning

You Can Manage Your Career

Some people have careers; most do not. People who drift from one job to another, doing this and that around town, do not have a career. They just have jobs.

The individual who decides to become a doctor or a lawyer or a CPA or a consulting engineer or an electrical engineer probably will have a career, perhaps not, depending upon how the person handles things. Someone who begins by selling books in the field and works up through editing into the management of a publishing company has a career.

Thus, when we talk about careers we are referring to individuals who decide to enter either one type of work, such as engineering or law or business, or who decide to begin in one industry and progress through it. This is not meant to imply that there are not successful individuals who, for one reason or another, change careers at some point during their lifetimes. Someone may begin by having a career in engineering, then switch to a management career. This is not to imply that only people with high-paying or top-level jobs have careers. A woman can be a career police officer; a man might be a career traffic manager. Both would fit well within the framework of what we are talking about. Career planning begins with your concept of your career. People who just have jobs don't do much planning.

You Can Determine Your Destiny

It is rather disturbing to encounter people who believe that their destinies are in the hands of the gods, who really believe that their lives are empty bottles tossed around on the seas of life. If you are such a person, you probably will not be reading this book. However, let us deal with this matter right now. It is critical to the rest of this work that you really believe that to a very great extent you determine your own destiny. The decisions you make in life greatly affect what happens to you. To a large extent, you can manage your career. If you do not believe this, you will find it exceedingly difficult to accept much of what follows. Because this point is so important, let's examine it.

The president of a large recruiting firm said, "Blind fate accounts for at least 60 percent of what happens in careers." But then the same article quotes a General Electric management development specialist as saying, "To a far greater degree than most people imagine, a career can be managed." Another top executive said, "People can never abdicate the fundamental responsibility of their own careers."[1]

Perhaps a bit of thought will resolve these two differing views of careers, for they are not truly opposites. Each speaker is correct if his words are carefully studied; they are talking about two different things. Fate does play a heavy hand in most careers, but that is because most people allow it to do so; they have no career plan, so they delegate their fates to the gods. People who do carefully plan their careers remove much of fate's leeway to play dice with their futures. People with no plans are most apt to allow whatever comes down the road to affect their lives. They go wherever the road leads them, for they have no set destination. The career planner knows the road of his choosing.

---

[1]"Plotting the Route to the Top," *Business Week*, October 12, 1974, p. 127.

Your first critical decision in career management is selecting the field you want to enter. Some people sentence themselves to a life of disappointment from the very beginning by making unwise career selections: (1) they choose careers for which there is a declining demand and in which success is unlikely; (2) they choose careers for which they are personally unsuited; or (3) they select careers that cannot provide them with what they seek.

DEMAND

For example, there are some fields in engineering in which the future demand for certain skills will be less than the supply of people with them; thus, competitive conditions will be exceedingly keen and many marginal people possessing such skills will be forced out of the field. One prime example comes to mind.

Rosie was a sandwich-maker at the Big Canyon Country Club in Newport Beach, California. She was a marvelous woman who possessed a great personality. Everyone in the club adored her. It was quite obvious from any casual conversation with her that she was a most intelligent woman. She had a master's degree in aeronautical engineering from Georgia Tech, and it so happened that her particular specialty was engineering propellers for aircraft. There just is not much demand for such talents today, and she was either unwilling or unable to make a transfer into other engineering fields. Hers was a career gone into the dust and a terrible waste of talent.

At all times in our society the demand for skills is changing; some are increasing in demand while others are declining. Thus, the decisions you make about which field to go into are exceedingly critical to your long-run success. If you select a career for which there is going to be ample demand in relationship to supply, the likelihood of your success is greatly increased.

Many people enjoy long and successful careers largely because they had the good foresight or good fortune to get into a rapidly growing industry. Ross Perot is only one of many people who have carved out fortunes from the computer service industry. He correctly foresaw that there would be a tremendous demand for computer software organizations.

Today, people going into such fields as solar energy, medical care, home maintenance services, and security would appear to have better than average prospects for rewarding careers.

INCOMPATIBILITY

And then there are the well-recognized cases of people selecting careers for which they simply are not suited. Give yourself a chance, a break! Why deliberately go into something for which you have neither the skills nor the liking?

Tom was told by many of his teachers and acquaintances that life insurance agents make lots of money. Tom wanted to make lots of money, so he proceeded to sell life insurance. He was miserable for he did not like the work, and later admitted that he did not particularly believe in the product, a sure formula for failure if there ever was one. At age thirty-four, he finally threw in the towel and decided to try something else. He left the field to go to work for an oil-field drilling company and is now following a noncareer pattern.

WORKING THE WRONG CLAIM

Kim sought a fortune in the women's apparel industry. She went to work for a department store chain and did an excellent job. After several promotions, it slowly dawned on her that the company could not provide her with the rewards she wanted. She discovered that the store could never pay her as much as she wanted to earn and that she really did not like either retailing or the apparel industry. Kim is now looking for a career in another industry while dutifully holding onto her job.

DECISIONS, DECISIONS, DECISIONS

Other critical decisions you make definitely affect your destiny. If you decide to get a college degree at a certain university, you increase your likelihood for a meaningful career. If you decide to attend the Harvard Graduate School of Business Administration (or one of similar standing), you have greatly increased your chances for success. The companies you decide to work for will play a critical role in your career. Work for the wrong concern and you may hurt yourself rather badly. Decide to cut a few corners by padding some expense accounts or lying on some reports and when you are discovered (and you will be discovered) your career will be affected. Business executives have an aversion to crooks, despite all the nonsense one can hear in jokes about padded expense accounts.

Hence, throughout your life you will make many critical decisions regarding what you are going to do, and each one of those decisions can make or break you. Thus, in a very real sense, you control your destiny by the wisdom with which you make decisions. For an extreme example, just think a moment about all the careers that were shattered by the Watergate affair. Many people made bad decisions and will pay for them for the rest of their lives. The price for some bad decisions can be frightful.

Career Planning

First off, let's admit that one's ability to plan is somewhat limited, since forecasting what lies over the horizon is impossible for any of us. You may step off a curb tomorrow and solve your entire career problem. You never know when you will wake up some morning and receive an offer that will set you off in an entirely different direction toward a most rewarding career. We admit all of these things. Nevertheless, there is great virtue in doing some planning so you can have some idea about where you are heading. Admittedly, such planning need only be sketchy; nevertheless, you will find that it will be of value.

Bruce was a young man contemplating going to college. He was fortunate in that he had a goal: to own a menswear store. He had the first requisite for making a plan—a goal he wanted to reach. Making plans when one is uncertain where one wants to go is difficult; however, it is not impossible. It just means that one's plans must allow flexibility and leave many options open. Bruce's plan was to attend college, major in marketing, then go to work for a manufacturer's representative in the men's apparel field. He could gain experience and exposure to all types of retail stores and learn how the various merchants operated. After three or four years' selling experience, he intended to open his own store. His plan included learning about the retail aspects of men's apparel merchandising by working in a men's store while he was in college.

Larry wanted to be an electrical engineer, so he planned to attend Purdue. Upon graduation, he would work for a small electronics company so that he could gain a wider range of experience than would probably be given him if he became a junior engineer in a large concern.

John was the son of the president of a very large textile manufacturer. Ultimately, he planned to go into the company to assume his hereditary role. However, his plan first called for working for several competitors. He could then bring a broader-based range of experience in how other companies were managed with him into his father's concern.

Gail was a senior majoring in marketing at a state university. She had no plan so she accepted the first job offer that was made to her, which proved to be a disaster. Then she got another job with a concern in a different industry, which proved to be equally disastrous. Thus began a noncareer of drifting from one job to another, never gaining enough expertise anywhere to be considered a professional. Gail considered herself a failure and could find no one to disagree with her. Without knowing what she was trying to put together, Gail simply did whatever was expedient when she had to do something. Expediency is a bad basis for making career decisions.

NEED FOR A PLAN IN MAKING DECISIONS

At various times you will be called upon to make critical decisions. Should you go to work for this company or that one? Should you do this or that? If you have a good plan, making such decisions will be facilitated. For example, if your plan ultimately calls for living in a small town and you want no part of big-city life, then it would be foolish to accept a job in a large corporation with a career path leading you to a home office in a large city. Unless your plan called for using that company only as a training base for a few years, it would be no place to develop the major thrust of your career.

Some of the decisions that you will be making are:

1. Should you take a job offer or not?
2. Should you change jobs?
3. Should you go to college?
4. If you go to school, what should be your major?
5. Where do you want to work?
6. For whom do you want to work?
7. What balance do you want to maintain between your career and home life?
8. Do you want to live in a big city or a small town?
9. Do you want to be in a business for yourself?

Skill Versus Luck

An ardent golfer sank a long putt, looked at his playing companions, and said, "I'll take luck and give skill every time." Everyone chuckled at that old bromide, but each of them knew better. Luck was not what dropped that putt for a birdie—it was largely skill. It was 90 percent skill, 10 percent luck, for he had to hit a good drive, hit the second shot onto the green, and be a good enough putter that he could give the ball a chance to drop.

The fact is (and never forget it) that skill will usually carry you through, but luck will desert you sooner or later. You cannot build a permanent career on luck. It takes skill to achieve success.

Now then, before you scream some objections that you know so-and-so who is in his position simply because he was lucky, we will hasten to agree with you. Many people have had considerable luck. It is most fortuitous if luck is combined with skill, but some people are just plain lucky. However, in the long run, luck tends to desert these people and in the end their careers reside in the ash can. Many top executives rise rapidly in a corporation on the basis of fortuitous circumstances, but when their skills are lacking, they fall even more rapidly.

Tim was an exceedingly personable young man who made a great name for himself selling consumer packaged goods. He soon became president of his concern, which was ultimately bought out by a large conglomerate which had heard of his prowess. He was one of America's wonder kids, or so the press tagged him. Made president of the larger company, Tim proceeded to make some of the most astounding business decisions imaginable, which ultimately proved disastrous to the company. He was unable to get a job in that industry thereafter and had to change careers. Luck took him to the top, but lack of skill brought him down.

Many of the people making big names in the financial pages, putting together this or that deal, are the beneficiaries of luck. They look great for a while as circumstances allow them to make millions. But note how many lose the dough even faster when their fortunes turn. When the real estate market in New York was great, William Zeckendorf looked like a genius. When the fortunes in the real estate market reversed . . . well, he did not look so good. Webb & Knapp went bankrupt. When money costs were low and the stock market high, Jim Ling looked great wheeling and dealing with one enterprise and another. But fortunes changed, as they always do. It took a different set of skills to succeed under different conditions. Thus, let us dispel once and for all the cop-out that your career is largely a matter of luck. When the football coaches tell you that a good team makes its own luck, they are not chanting locker room oratory. You make your own luck!

Need for Preparation

You should not delude yourself into thinking that you can manage to make a career from nothing. You have to prepare yourself for your career, and a great deal of your success will depend upon how well you do it. People who are truly great prepared themselves for their careers, perhaps for decades. General Patton was not a successful general overnight. He prepared himself over a lifetime for his great victories.

John was an executive vice-president of a defense electronics firm. He was a most able and successful director of research and was highly esteemed by everyone who knew him. He had that rare combination of engineering capabilities combined with an imaginative mind and administrative talents. John did not come by these accidentally. He spent a lifetime preparing himself for his position, not only by his engineering training but also by developing his managerial and creative skills.

Bill has a Ph.D. in chemistry from perhaps the leading university for such training. After a short but outstanding career in the laboratory, he was made director of research for a large organization and supervisor of 500 people. He did not come by this managerial position accidentally. He prepared himself very diligently over a period of years, not only by reading and by studying management intensively, but also by accepting a job teaching management at a university to further his understanding of that field.

You must prepare yourself. The better your preparation, the more likely is your success. One story on the importance of preparation was told by a football player reminiscing about playing under Coach Bud Wilkinson in Oklahoma's great days in the mid-fifties. He said that he never got over his amazement at Coach Wilkinson's preparation and attention to details. He anticipated and took care of every possibility. A study of the great coaches indicates that they have this trait in common to a certain degree. They believe in preparing their teams ahead of time to such an extent that on game day little is left to chance.

Careers in the Dust

One of the reasons that I have wanted for so long to write this book and feel so very strongly about this topic is the terrible tragedies I have seen in dealing with people who have come to me for help when their careers are lying in the dust. We do not have the space to go into the cases, nor is it really necessary, for they all would sound about the same. Their ages may be anywhere from thirty upward to fifty years old, but the stories are just about the same. I'll get a telephone call and the voice on the other end will say, "Professor, this is so-and-so. You probably don't remember me, but I was in one of your classes back at the University and I'd like to talk with you. Can I come and see you now?" There is always an urgency to it; they want to come out to the house right now. I know what is coming, and the story is usually quite grim. They have been working for a company or perhaps several companies and have gone nowhere. They have not been promoted nor have they had much success. Now they are out of a job, perhaps because they have been fired or laid off. Some of them have become fed up and resigned (a terrible mistake). They want advice on what they should do now.

These sessions usually take several hours, during which it is all the individual can do to keep from crying. He has had to swallow a lot of pride to see the old prof and admit his failure, but he is desperate—he is at the end of his rope.

These people still desperately seek the success that has eluded them. They simply do not know what to do, yet they are not willing to throw in the towel and call it quits. Unquestionably, they know their careers are in the dust, and they want to recover somehow. It does not happen often, but every once in a while some of these people can be saved.

Incidentally, if at this point you wonder what their basic problems are, it is usually that their career expectations greatly exceeded their capabilities. They were almost doomed to failure from the beginning because they expected far more than their skills would allow them to obtain. Of course, this is a touchy, difficult obstacle to overcome, to get a person to base a career plan on reasonable expectations. We simply must realize that not everyone can be president of a large corporation. Even more frustrating are the people blessed with talent who have climbed the ladder of success only to fall off because of some foolish tactical career blunder.

Moss was a handsome man of regal bearing who was most impressive upon meeting, so impressive that he rapidly rose to the presidency of a major corporation by the tender age of thirty-five. He was a "boy wonder" of business. His career was envied by all. Unfortunately, he blew his success by reaching too high and losing it all.

Moss made a strong bid for the chairmanship of the board of the company but unfortunately, he had furnished his adversary for the top job with the ammunition to shoot him down. All had not been going well in one of Moss' key operating companies. It was losing money—$10 million in the last year. Since Moss had not been doing much about it he hardly had the credentials for a promotion. Moss lost his bid for the top job and the man who beat him made a point of firing Moss upon ascension into power. Moss caught on at another famous company but was unseated from power in three months when the organization discovered he knew little about the business. He had forgotten that it takes more than appearance to keep your job. He had not learned on his way up how to manage companies.

Thus, one of the objectives of this book is to try to help you so you will not find yourself down the road with a career that has gone sour.

Goals

One common factor noted in the career planning of succesful people is that in most cases they knew what they wanted—they had goals. One top executive for a large industrial goods manufacturer, when asked to what he attributed his success, replied, "I made up my mind what I wanted and went out and got it." It seems to be a matter of making up your mind what you want to do and then making it happen. Successful people make it happen, but without goals you do not know what you want to happen, so nothing good is likely to come about.

Joe, a successful men's apparel merchant, knew from the time he was a sophomore in high school that he wanted to have his own menswear store. He never thought he would be anything else but a haberdasher. He prepared for the task by going to college and studying merchandising while working in a men's apparel store. Upon graduation he went to work for a large department store in the menswear department until he felt capable of opening his own store. Once he had made up his mind that the time was right, he opened a store, and it was most successful. Even during his time in the Army, he spent his furloughs surveying likely towns for store sites. His mind was seldom off his goal.

Tom, while in college, did not really know what he wanted to do. During his senior year he worked in a high-class restaurant and enjoyed it. He decided he wanted to own such an establishment, so he set about learning the business. He became the successful owner of a large chain of restaurants. Nothing happened to Tom until he set his goals. Once his goal was set, he had the key to advancement.

All of this sounds so simple, but it is far from it. Many people just do not know what they really want to do. They let fate deal the cards; whatever turns up decides the direction of their lives. Many college seniors have only a vague idea of their goals. Typically, they take interviews with a wide range of companies, listen to all the stories, then go to work for the company that has sent out the best liar. Now that's no way to run a railroad! Small wonder that the turnover of college graduates on their first jobs is so high. They do not really select the job nor is the job taken with much of a plan in mind! Rather, they place their careers in the hands of job sales reps who are being paid to tell them fanciful stories about the wonders of their companies.

Let's spend a while talking about how to attack the problem of having no goal. If you have a goal, then you do not have that problem. You know what you want, so go get it.

Attacking the No-Goal Problem

Experience—get it! Most college seniors who do not know what they want to do have one thing in common: they have not had the experience that would allow them to discover what they like and dislike. Seldom have they held any meaningful jobs; many have never had one at all. They have not talked with many people of interest. In short, they simply do not have enough experience in life to know what they want to do.

The younger generation suffers from the overly protective labor laws that have discouraged, even prevented, them from gaining much needed experience. Indeed, many illustrious careers were nurtured at very tender ages.

If you lack experience, then the only solution is to go get some. Go to work whether you need to or not. Go out of your way to talk to people about their jobs in a wide range of occupations, how they like the work, and what they do. Pump people about their careers. One young man realized that he desperately needed some on-the-job experience. So he walked into a certain firm that could provide it and volunteered to work without pay in exchange for being taught what he wanted to know. Remember, experience does not come wandering in your door. You must go out and grab it off the street.

WHAT TURNS YOU ON?

Nothing at all is wrong with basing your career on your personal likes and dislikes. What turns you on in life? Do you really enjoy music? Then perhaps one of the many careers in the music industry would appeal to you. Are you a ski bum? Well, there are jobs in the skiing industry. A young man recently became a lawyer. He was also a ski bum so he decided to practice his calling in Mammouth, California, so that he would be next to his beloved slopes. A good doctor should like the field of medicine; a good lawyer enjoys the law. It has been said time and again that people who are successful in their careers like what they are doing—it turns them on. Well then, start looking for a career among activities you enjoy.

THE NINE-FACTOR ANALYSIS

If you will but answer the following nine questions honestly and in detail, you may find the answers will help you in making a decision about your goals.

  1. How much money do you really need to consider yourself successful?

  If nothing but big money will satisfy you, then you will have to begin thinking about owning your own business, for it is most unlikely that large sums will come your way while working for other people. On the other hand, if you can be happy working for the wages paid by companies for the position you have in mind, then those paths can be used. This point seems so simple, but it causes so much distress.

  A sales representative for a pattern publishing company became unhappy after several years of excellent performance because her salary had reached a plateau at $15,000 a year. She wanted more, much more. When she learned that even her managers were not earning as much as she wanted, she quit and went into real estate—a field that could give her the money she wanted.

Make some money decisions, serious ones, without wishful thinking, pie-in-the-sky dreams. Once you have decided what you *must* earn, then shun career paths unlikely to provide it.

While average pay scales are interesting, even more important are the wages paid to the top 10 to 20 percent of the people in some callings. In many fields the average wage and the top wage are not all that far apart; the succesful person has nowhere to go. Teaching is one such field. The beginning assistant professor teaching in 1979 earns about $19,500. A thirty-year full professor at the same institution earns about $27,000. That is not much for a young person to look forward to earning. On the other hand, there are fields in which the average wages are low but the top salaries paid are quite high. Retailing is one such field. One top-notch men's apparel organization, The Regiment Shops of Colorado, starts its salespeople at $1,000 per month but within two years that person will be earning $25,000 a year. If the individual has management potential, a promotion into store management will bring $40,000 to $60,000 into the family coffers. The owners of the chain earn six-figure incomes. Now that kind of a situation holds promise to a young person on the make.

2. *What kind of work do you really want to do?*

Some people want to work alone with figures or at a drawing board; others want to work with other people. Some persons like desk jobs; others want to be in the field. Other individuals are unhappy unless they are actually building or creating something.

Your Career

A prime example would be the resignation of John Z. DeLorian as a top executive of General Motors. Evidently Mr. DeLorian was a most talented individual, for he rose rapidly to manage the Chevrolet Division. His success promoted him into GM top management, from which he rather quickly resigned. According to industry sources, he found the job in top management to be frustrating and unrewarding in comparison to his former job. As the boss of Chevrolet he was in the midst of operations, making numerous decisions regarding the manufacture and distribution of automobiles. He could get things done; he could issue orders. It was a satisfying job. In GM top management he was spending most of his time in committee work. He issued no direct orders nor could he really see the results of his efforts. He simply was not receiving the job satisfactions he wanted. It was not the type of work he wanted to do. He now has started his own car company in Ireland.

Harvey was an excellent mechanical engineer who wanted to progress into top management, and his talents allowed him to do so. However, the higher he rose, the less he had to do with engineering and the more he had to do with management. One day he discovered that his job had nothing to do with engineering and that he was involved up to his eyeballs in all the problems of managing people, whereupon he resigned and accepted another job doing what he really enjoyed. He discovered he did not like being a manager.

One young man harbored thoughts of becoming a mining engineer until he discovered that most such jobs were in remote, small mining towns. Such a life held no appeal for him, so he chose another career. In another case a young woman planned a career in fashion merchandising until she discovered the amount of paperwork needed and the long hours and weekend work that are frequently required.

If you do not like detail work or working with numbers, then do not think about becoming a CPA. If you do not really enjoy caring for people, then perhaps you would be better off not going into medicine. It is that simple, but for some reason many of these simple things that are so important to careers are overlooked in our planning.

3. *What type of environment do you want?*

Max found himself in an embarrassing predicament: With only a high school diploma, he took a job working in the warehouse for a General Motors Wholesale Parts Division. He started at the bottom of the ladder. Five years later he was manager for General Motors Wholesale Parts Division selling to independent dealers in the Rocky Mountain area. Evidently Max was quite good at his job, for he was offered a promotion to head up the wholesaling of parts to independent dealers all over the nation. This required moving from Denver to Detroit. He and his family were greatly distressed, for they did not want to leave Denver, particularly for Detroit. He turned down the promotion and eventually resigned his position. If you do not want to work and live in a large city, then do not go to work for a company whose home office is there. More will be said of this point later, but it is quite important in setting your goals that you make some decisions about the environment in which you want to work and live.

Absolutely nothing is wrong with making a career decision on the basis of where you want to live. But be warned, don't weep later about how your choice of living conditions has limited your mobility and choice of jobs. You'll have little choice in selecting a company to work for if there is but one employer in the area where you want to live.

4. What are the social needs of yourself and your family?

Some people want to lead an active social life in the broadest sense of the word; they simply want to spend a large portion of their time doing something other than working and pursuing academic endeavors. Some careers demand an almost total dedication to work. Many physicians, for example, have little time for social endeavors. Many top executives spend every waking hour concerned with business affairs. If you do not want to lead that type of life, then do not start down that trail.

5. What kind of family life do you want to lead?

Closely akin to the previous considerations, some careers leave little or no time for one's family. If you will recall the hero in *The Man in the Gray Flannel Suit,* who opted for a richer family life in lieu of a successful career in top management, you have an example of this type of decision. Each career poses different demands upon the individual that directly affect the type of family life he or she is allowed to have. Some physicians choose to specialize in pathology rather than in obstetrics or orthopedic surgery because they can work when they please rather than when the patient needs them. This way they gain more freedom.

6. How much prestige does your ego require?

There is no sweeping under the rug the fact that careers vary immensely in the prestige that they bestow upon their followers. There is a pecking order among the professions. Physicians are typically awarded positions of high prestige. The vice-presidency of a bank is usually considered a more prestigious position than the vice-presidency of a small manufacturing company. Surprisingly, money does not have a great deal to do with this matter of prestige. The branch manager of a bank making $20,000 a year may have far more prestige than the owner of a lemonade stand at a fair who nets $100,000 a year.

One of the problems encountered in managing The Regiment Shops of Colorado was the difficulty of attracting talented individuals to work as salespeople despite the attractive pay. Their egos just could not accept the low status bestowed upon retail salespeople by society. If prestige is your bag, or if your spouse really wants you to do something that he or she is not ashamed to talk about, then you had better take this into consideration in your selection of goals.

Ernie had a chance to buy a most profitable rubbish removal company for an attractive price. From conservative estimates, he would have made more than $75,000 a year from the enterprise above his payout to the owner. His wife refused to go along with the plan because she could not stand the thought of being married to a garbage collector. Prestige can be most expensive! However, if such things are important to you (and they are to most people), then you must take them into consideration in setting your goals.

7. How much security must you have?

Some people do not want to take chances. They want to minimize their risks. Some opt for civil service, others go into teaching or working for very large corporations in the hope that they will not have to worry about being out of a job. One of the traditional appeals of being a white-collar worker rather than a blue-collar worker was that white-collar work offered more security. Certain occupations are more secure than others. If one goes into medicine or teaching, security risks are minimized. People who decide to run their own enterprises admittedly are undertaking hazardous careers. Some personalities cannot live with conditions of uncertainty or ambiguity.

Such people should not be in their own businesses, for psychologically they will not be able to tolerate the risks they are forced to encounter.

8. *What are your talents?*

What are you good at doing? What do you do poorly? One of the keys to being a winner is to do things that you are good at doing so you can have a reasonable chance to win. Brad was good at several things but sports was not one of them. Yet he spent all his time trying to be the great football player. In four years at Indiana University he did not get into a game. He was a loser as he always opted for games for which he was ill suited.

A brutally accurate appraisal of your talents can be most helpful in setting your goals. The choice is most simple—stay away from things you do poorly.

9. *What is the price you have to pay to reach possible goals?*

You must pay a price to achieve anything worthwhile. Thousands of young people enamored of a professional sports career fall by the wayside each year as they discover they don't want to pay the price for success in that activity. Sometimes the price is pain and effort, sometimes it is years in training, sometimes it is money. Whatever the price, if you're not willing to pay it, you'll not reach your goal. So try to appraise as honestly as you can what prices you must pay to reach the potential goals you are examining.

Changing Goals

There is nothing sacred about your goals. You can change them whenever you see the need to do so, and you should have no guilt feelings about it, for almost everyone changes. People mature, experience, learn, and change their values, all of which can affect their goals.

Admittedly, others begin to wonder about the stability of someone whose goals change more often than the weather. Somewhere along the line one must stay with one set of goals long enough to make some headway toward reaching them.

However, a new phenomenon has developed in recent years that has seized the imagination of many people: the so-called second career. Somewhere down the line the person decides that happiness can better be found doing something else. A drastic change of goals is then forthcoming. It is a daring move, particularly for those people who are successful in what they are doing. There is much to lose when all does not go well with the second career. One cannot help but wonder if many of these people could have been spared much of their agony had they but given more thought to the goals they really wanted to achieve when they started out. It might be added here that so far the experience of those people who have undertaken the second career strategy has not been encouraging.

Conflicting Goals

So far, this topic of goals has been largely a matter of deciding what it is you really want to do, but that is only the beginning. Once you have selected your goals, another problem raises its ugly head: what to do in a situation in which an action conflicts with one goal while satisfying another.

Dave D., age fifty, was a consulting engineer of some repute who lived and worked in Palo Alto, California. He had just completed the first year of a four-year contract with a large electronics manufacturer to do a study that he found to be quite interesting. The total value of the contract was $100,000 ($25,000 a year). At this stage in life, Dave had a fairly good handle on his goals, which were: to live in a pleasant environment (Dave and his family liked California); to obtain a secure source of relatively good income; to do interesting work; and to have considerable leisure time. His electronics contract met all the goals except the one concerning a good, secure income. He was apprehensive about his future at the end of the contract. Business conditions did not look good and he was getting old. He had an offer of a tenured professorship from a university in a large southern town that met all of his goals but the one concerned with living conditions. He and his family were not enthralled with moving to that particular city.

Thus the classic problem is posed: a person's goals conflict with each other. Something has to give. Either Dave will have to forget about environment or forget about security. Incidentally, he opted for security, saying, "We can't eat climate."

You must decide what is really most important to you because you will continually be tested by opportunities that conflict in some way with your goals. In Dave's case, he reasoned, "We can get along okay without interesting work, in a poor environment, and without a lot of leisure, but there is no way we can make it without a secure income."

You should classify your goals in three groups:

1. No-compromise, "must-happen" goals.
2. Important but nonessential goals.
3. Nice-to-have goals, but let us not get led astray and go after these at the expense of the goals in groups 1 and 2.

Strategy

Some valuable things, such as diamonds, come in small packages. Career strategy is one of these things. It is a relatively simple concept, still it is an exceedingly important one for you to consider. In the decision-making models currently in vogue, after establishing your goals, you then select a strategy for reaching them. While strategy sounds like a profound bit of thinking, it is but a fancy word for a plan. A strategy is a plan of action. It is how one intends to reach a goal. Experience has shown that if one does not have some plan in mind for achieving one's goals in life, one is not apt to reach them. Goal achievement is not likely to happen by accident. It is difficult enough to achieve one's goals with a plan; without one it is not likely to happen.

Jim L. was a young man with an exceptionally bright mind and a technical leaning. After graduating from Purdue with highest honors in mechanics, he accepted employment with a large machinery manufacturer because it seemed to be the best thing on the horizon. Jim worked for that concern for several years and then was enticed away by an aerospace concern offering considerably more money. All went well for Jim for three years until the aerospace firm lost its defense contract and had to cut back. You know the story. After ten months of anguish Jim finally latched onto an engineering job for a small computer company in Santa Ana, California, designing various mechanical devices connected with computers. Jim was now thirty-seven years old and beginning to ask some questions, such as, "Where in the world am I going?" "What's going to become of me?" "What do I really want to be?"

The problem was that Jim had been drifting on the sea of economic opportunity and had simply gone whichever way the tide had taken him. He had no plan. His goals were a vague desire for monetary success and a position with a well-established firm. He wanted to become a responsible manager, but he had no plan for getting there.

The Need for a Plan

There are three major reasons why you need a plan—some plan—at all times. First, all sorts of unexpected events arise about which a decision must be made. Someone you meet offers you a job. Without a plan you won't have anything against which to measure those opportunities, thus you can be lured into unproductive traps. If you know what you want and have a plan for getting it, then when someone offers you something you can compare that offer against your plan to see if it fits. If it does not fit, you can either reject the offer or reconsider your plan. More will be said about the latter in the next section.

Second, a plan provides some emotional peace of mind. People worry about their careers, worry about what will become of them and what the future holds. The person who has a plan for getting what he wants is apt to feel more secure and less apt to worry about things. Time and again I am impressed that people who seek career advice seem genuinely disturbed because they have no plan for their lives. They do not know where they are going. They vaguely know what they want, but they are not quite sure about how to get it. Thus there is value in having a plan that gives you some idea of where you want to go and how you are going to get there.

Third, a plan is a yardstick by which you can judge how well you are doing. If you have set forth a detailed plan with a timetable, then you have a basis for comparing your progress. At any time you can compare your progress with what you had planned to do. Then some terrible questions can arise if your progress is unsatisfactory: Was the plan too ambitious? Does it need modifying? Can anything be done to hasten progress to catch up with the plan?

Change in Plans

Let us not be naive. Seldom does anyone go through life without changing plans. We have seen how goals change, thus requiring changes in plans; however, people also change plans for reaching the same goals.

Many times opportunities arise making a change of plans necessary. A young woman accepted employment with a department store with the thought of staying with that store to become merchandising manager. She wanted to learn the operation. Her plan was to remain with the same firm and work her way up through management. She was well on her way when suddenly she had a particularly attractive offer to manage and own a substantial part of a large specialty store. She changed goals and plans. Managing the large specialty store seemed a suitable substitute for merchandising manager of the department store, so she accepted it. Basically, her goal was to be in a position of authority to run a merchandising operation.

Sometimes plans change because of happenstance and changing fortunes. A vice-president of a large paint company was on his way toward top management when his heart condition made him change plans. Perhaps the economy sours, thus plans for going into one's own business must be postponed. Perhaps an inheritance one was counting on fails to materialize, thus causing a change in retirement plans. Whatever, one's voyage through life weathers many storms necessitating changes in course.

There is the matter of values. People change plans simply because they change values or philosophies of life. One successful corporate executive suddenly tired of the rat race and developed a small concern in Dallas, called Servit, that installs and services home beverage dispensers. He is happy today because he likes what he is doing. A few people do escape the "rat race."

As we can see, many plan changes are caused by basic changes in one's goals, but some are simply a reappraisal of the best way to reach the same goal.

Examples

Strategy is a word with glittering generality—sounds great, but exactly what does it mean? It is difficult to define the word *strategy*, for people project into it all sorts of meanings. The best way to defuzz the word is to provide you with some examples of strategy in action. Let's look at some people.

The case of Joe, mentioned several times previously, is illustrative of many good aspects of career management, but in particular his strategy was exceptionally sound. Joe was the man who, at the age of fifteen, had planned to become a haberdasher. His goal was firmly and clearly in mind. The strategy he formulated at that young age was first to attend the state university and obtain a degree in marketing, which he did. He particularly stressed all courses connected with retailing. Then he planned to work for a short time in the men's department of a large department store while awaiting a call to the armed forces, which he did. Since he was an officer in the reserve, he spent his available spare time in the service surveying college campuses in various areas for likely locations for his men's store. He spent two years looking at practically every major college campus in the nation, all according to plan. He finally selected one and, upon discharge from the service, opened a store in Boulder, Colorado that was a success from the start.

Betty wanted to become a college professor because her father had been one and she had come to appreciate many of the advantages the profession offered. Her strategy was as follows. First, obtain a bachelor's degree from a major university. Second, go out and work for two years to get experience in the particular field of her interest. Third, return to school for graduate work. Her plan was to seek an M.S. in finance rather than an M.B.A. because she felt that the M.B.A. was more suitable for aspiring business executives. An M.S. in finance would provide a better preparation for a Ph.D. in finance and for teaching the subject. The Ph.D. was to be obtained from a Big-10 university in order to facilitate her marketability. The university was chosen because of her particular personal and financial realities.

It is rather interesting to note the number of young men and women who have come to SMU because of its position in the entrepreneurship arena. My graduate assistant in 1974, a Notre Dame alumnus, had as his goal to become a management consultant. He wanted to work with some firms such as Booz, Allen & Hamilton, or McKinsey & Company. He felt it was more likely that he would gain the consulting experience he needed in an action learning situation where the students do a great deal of consulting work than if he attended a school where the classes are conducted in a more traditional lecture format. Currently Terry is heading up a consulting project for an oil company which, in the end, will give him unquestionably excellent credentials for work in management consulting. An update on Terry's progress five years later is illustrative of several points. The oil company offered him a good job (he was the highest-paid graduate in the class) in buying steel pipe (casing). After a year dealing in steel pipe, he started his own business as a steel pipe broker and is doing exceptionally well.

The following is a quote about Tom Wilscam from an article about his rise to fame and fortune in the restaurant business.[2] Note his strategy in action.

Wilscam was not immediately successful off the gridiron. When he graduated in 1961, neither his journalism degree nor his football record brought him the advertising job he wanted. "It was the old story—no experience, no job," he says.

But in football, as he pointed out, if you can't move toward the goal in a straight line, you go wherever there is an opening.

So he accepted the first offer, although it did not excite him. The owner of a Boulder restaurant in which Tom had been working as a parttime waiter offered him a chance to manage the place.

"I'd never even thought about the restaurant business as a career," Wilscam says, "but I found out I had a talent for it. I talked to the kitchen workers as if they were a team, and the food and service improved. I tripled the business in four months. So I decided to go into this busi-

---

[2]Olga Curtis, "Whatever Happened to CU's Other Guard?" *Empire Magazine,* January 19, 1975, p. 8.

---

ness for the same reason I went into football—because I was good at it."

The restaurant then admired most was the Alpine Village in Denver. Wilscam decided to open a similar German-style restaurant in Boulder and asked Fred Mikawa, a CU architecture student, to draw up the plans. (Mikawa, who has designed all of Wilscam's restaurants, is now a vice-president of Wilscam Enterprises.)

But Tom could not find any backers. "I went to two businessmen who knew me as a CU player," he says. "Every one of them pointed out the restaurant business had the highest mortality rate of any business, that I only had four months' experience and that I really didn't know much about the economics of the thing."

Tenacious Tom asked the owner of the Alpine Village Inn, the late Ray Dambach, for a job. When Dambach said there were no openings, Wilscam offered to work for nothing. Dambach agreed.

For the next seven months Wilscam worked as a laborer in the mornings, and spent afternoons and evenings working for no pay in the restaurant. He started in the kitchen, peeling potatoes, and worked every job from waiter to bookkeeper to second cook.

"Dambach took me under his wing. He taught me everything he could. In the middle of 1962 he told me he was opening a restaurant on South Santa Fe Drive and would put me in as manager with 20 percent of net receipts."

Wilscam ran the Northwoods Inn so well that his 20 percent came to $14,000 a year. But he still wanted a restaurant of his own and spent a lot of time planning it. He explains, "There is a general idea that anyone can open a restaurant, that all you need is a wife who can cook. But success in the restaurant business depends on the public, and people don't go to restaurants just to eat. They go for

psychological reasons, romance, or escape or good fel-
lowship. So you have to provide atmosphere as well as
good food and good service. Otherwise you could serve
the same food in a gym, but people wouldn't enjoy it."

I wish I could report all was well with Tom, but he fell
upon hard times as he proved unable to control a multi-
unit restaurant operation. His strategy was sound and he
reached his goals initially, but lost success because he
overlooked the fact that once you reach the top you have
to work even harder to stay there. Success is not the doorway to easy living.

Ross, a bright mechanical engineer with a Georgia
Tech pedigree, had a goal to become vice-president of
manufacturing for some medium-sized manufacturer.
He embarked upon a strategy that had him accept employment with a large consulting firm. He reasoned that
with the consulting firm he would be exposed to a large
number of manufacturing situations that needed help in
the production area. Why else would they be coming to a
consultant for help if they didn't need it? From this exposure he felt that he would be able to spot a position to
his liking. He did! That is strategy.

Diane wanted to go into politics. She had aspirations
for power and a morality that allowed it. Her strategy
was first to obtain a law degree from the state university,
then run for district attorney so that everyone in the area
would learn her name. After all, the district attorney's
name is constantly appearing in the newspapers in connection with many cases and thus has a great deal of visi-
bility. Then Diane planned to run for the state legislature,
all the time playing a big role in Democratic party politics. Presently she is right on schedule. Oh yes, the ultimate goal behind all her political maneuvering was
simply to build up a lucrative law practice, which she has.

Your Personal Development

While walking around with Hale Irwin, 1974 and 1979 U.S. Open Champion, during the Pro-Am of the 1972 Los Angeles Open, I overheard a man in the gallery exclaim, "Gee, it must be wonderful to have all that natural talent and be able to play golf that way without effort."

What nonsense, I thought, for I had watched Hale spend countless hours at the Boulder Country Club hitting golf balls and working diligently on his game. He worked extremely hard and studied the game carefully to reach the pinnacle of success. One night in 1969 while riding to Denver, we were talking about his forthcoming career on the pro circuit and he said, "I know that I can be successful on the tour, but it's going to take me about five years to learn and develop my game under tough competition."

Here was a man who at that time could hit a golf ball just about any place he wanted and who was already the NCAA Golf Champion, yet he recognized that he needed to apply himself diligently by studying and developing himself if he was to achieve the success he sought. In all professional sports highly skilled rookies recognize that they still must spend perhaps several years perfecting their skills before they will be able to compete with the veterans.

Some people think that the stars in the entertainment world achieve success overnight by being "discovered in Schwab's." Don't believe it. Conversation after conversation with such people clearly shows that they spend many years of hard work studying their craft and perfecting their techniques. Indeed, in the heyday of MGM, the company spent countless millions schooling their stars in all aspects of the art much the same way as IBM hires young people fresh out of college and trains them to sell computers. MGM would put a promising body under contract and then train it in dramatics, dancing, singing, and sometimes, reading and writing. For this reason many stars reached stardom relatively late in life. It takes time to master an art.

Encountering a young college graduate who feels ready to assume the reins of the presidency of some large corporation never ceases to be a source of some consternation. It just does not work that way. You will have to spend much time and exert a great deal of effort developing yourself. If you are unwilling to pay that price, then forget about success. You will not likely find it!

The Six Segments of Your Developmental Program

First, there is the matter of one's formal education. Unquestionably, today most successful careers are founded upon a good formal education that includes a college degree. Indeed, many professions (law, medicine, engineering, CPA) require college degrees, even advanced degrees. A great deal of thought should be given to such matters as:

What college should I attend?

What subject should I study?

Should I seek an advanced degree?

If so, when?

We will go into these matters in some detail shortly. However, formal education does not stop upon graduation from college. Most likely you will be involved in various educational programs for most of your professional life. Knowledge is expanding so rapidly in all fields that few people can continue to be competent without continual training.

Second, experience is certainly part of your development program. Working for someone who knows something that you want to learn makes sense, solely for that reason. When you are being considered for some prize position, rest assured that the experience you have previously acquired is by far one of the most important considerations. Thus your first few jobs are critical. If they are with the right people, future employers will take more interest in you than if you have been working places where little was to be learned.

A large manufacturer of store fixtures was seeking a new sales manager. Bill M., a young man of considerable proven talent, was strongly recommended for the job; he was the organization's choice for the opening. However, the president vetoed hiring Bill. "Look at the rinky-dink outfits he's been with. He's never been any place where he could learn what he needs to know for our job!" The president was wrong in this instance, but nevertheless he judged by past experience. With the right experience, your advancement will be much easier.

Third, your continual reading program is essential and some thought should be given to it. You will have to get much of your future education by reading books and trade magazines.

Fourth, you need to learn how to manage people, how to be an administrator. While this topic certainly overlaps the first three, still it is so important that we must give special consideration to how you can develop administrative skills.

Fifth, work at perfection in your personal attributes such as speaking habits, appearance, and behavior. While these may sound banal, and many people put them down in these days of the slob, many good job opportunities have been lost because the person's appearance was less than desired. Appearance is learned; you can develop it.

Sixth, emotional maturity is essential for people who seek high positions, so some thoughts will be given about how you might develop emotionally.

About Colleges

"All colleges are about the same. It really doesn't matter which one you go to. The important thing is to get the degree." So claimed a student at a degree mill that had best be unnamed. Don't you believe it! It does make a difference. But before we open up that can of worms, the question needs to be asked:

SHOULD YOU GO TO COLLEGE?

The answer depends upon you and your career goals. Certain careers require a college degree, others do not. It is foolish to try to buck the odds. If a degree is needed, get it.

Frieda W., after getting her masters degree, discovered that she was a great college teacher. She liked it and her students loved her, but without a doctorate a college professor's career is most limited. Frieda refused, for some reason buried deep in her mind, to get her doctorate. She is now fifty years old and is unhappy with a career that has gone nowhere.

Don't fight it. Get whatever credentials are needed for what you want to do. Success is difficult enough to achieve without foolishly placing unnecessary barriers in your path. Without credentials, success becomes remote.

If college training or a degree is not needed for the career you have selected, still you may be wise to consider two things. First, you may decide later to change your goal, or discover something else that you would like to do better. And that "something else" may require college training. Yet for you the boat may have sailed. For many reasons, you might find it most difficult to go back to school at an older age. A college degree gives you more options. You have more careers open to you. Without the degree, you burn a certain number of bridges before you come to them.

Perhaps Matt's tale illustrates the point. Matt was a normally bright lad who forsook college in favor of marriage and a job as a milkman right out of high school. He and his wife were happy. Matt made good money; they lived far better than their contemporaries, at least at first. But things changed. At the 10-year reunion of their high school class Matt noticed that many of his classmates had now passed him by and that he had gone nowhere. At the 15-year reunion he talked meekly about going back to school to get into something better, but then he would mumble something about not being able to do so because of his responsibilities. At the 25th reunion Matt was a beaten man; he did not show up. A talk with him disclosed a bitter man. Other classmates whom he considered inferior had brilliant careers; his was a failure.

Then there is the matter of basic career strategy. Many career experts feel strongly that a person should try to keep open as many options as possible, particularly if the person is not altogether certain what he or she wants to do. The lack of good college training and a degree certainly limits one's career choices in this technological age. (Note: good training and a degree are not the same thing; there are many degrees that are almost worthless.)

WHICH COLLEGE?

Time and again the author is asked which schools are the "best." The answer is, it all depends upon:

What you want to study

Your finances

Where you want to live

Your abilities

How hard you want to work

Your aspirations

Your contacts and friends

How you feel about the schools

And, no doubt, a dozen other personal factors.

However, schools unquestionably do have images, and people generally judge one's education by the schools attended. Some bum who spends four years loafing through an esteemed Ivy League school with little to show for the money will still be considered by most people to have a far superior education to that of a bright person who gained excellent training at some school considered a low-status institution. One's record does not really show the quality of one's education. People judge by images—admittedly a terrible situation, but that is the way the cards are dealt.

What we have been talking about to this point is a matter of appearances, not reality. Without question, many people go to some college that is not renowned for the excellence of its programs and are fortunate enough to encounter some particularly adept professor with whom an excellent rapport is established. In such circumstances, that individual will get a far superior education than most people obtain at the famous schools. Ironically, one or two excellent professors can make all the difference in the world to your personal development. However, this is in the realm of reality. These learning experiences do not show up on your transcript or your resume. Only you know how much you learned; the public has only appearances on which to rely. It is assumed that the excellence of your education will show up on your first job, but you have to get one first, which brings us to the matter of just what excellent academic credentials will do for you.

Credentials do not ensure success. About all a college degree will do is to qualify you for your first job. Indeed, many times it will get your first job for you. A Harvard M.B.A. degree will get you a good job; there is no doubt about that. But many other schools also have excellent placement capabilities. The degree can get you started, but thereafter what you do on the job becomes more and more important until about age forty when the degree does not have much significance at all. At that point, you have a sufficient track record so that potential employers are going to look at your accomplishments and not where you went to school in making their decisions about you. Indeed, if you have a Harvard M.B.A. and at age forty are not successful, that fact alone may block getting a job, for the potential employer will have good reason to question your abilities.

When pressed hard for an answer by someone who really has a need for honest advice, the author replies, "If you can afford it, go to the university with the best general image among the people in the city where you want to live, for the profession you wish to pursue. If you can't afford it, don't worry about it. You can get a better education elsewhere. The image problem is no real barrier to the talented person."

A bothersome conclusion can come from that advice: "The less talent one has, the more important it is to go to a prestigious school." So we must hasten to point out the opposite truth. Some people possess great potential for some calling that needs a great education and a few schools are so outstanding in that field that the individual should make every effort to attend one of them, for the additional benefits are unquestionable. If you have musical talent you would try to go to Juilliard. A scientist would try to get into Cal Tech or MIT. Those who want to be top-flight lawyers try to attend Harvard, Yale, Stanford, or Michigan. There are a number of top-notch engineering schools, some particularly good in one specialty while others are better in another.

But we have been talking about only an extremely small percentage of our work force. The average person has to go to some affordable school that is near home. Try to find a school that is respectable in the subject area of your interest. Try to talk with some of the more mature students who attend the college you are considering. Try to find out the school's attrition rate. Do their students stick around and graduate?

EXPERIENCE VERSUS COLLEGE

In early 1974 my son brought home a friend who was seeking advice for a problem. The lad was graduating from high school and was down for the weekend on the USC campus to look it over. He was staying at my son's fraternity house. One thing led to another and they came to see what the old man had to say about it. Here is the story.

"My father doesn't want me to go to college. He thinks it's a waste of time. He has offered to give me $10,000 and I can either use it for college or to set up a hobby shop. That's really what I want to do, own a hobby shop." I asked the young man if he knew much about running a hobby shop; he replied that he did not. He seemed to be a bright, ambitious lad. We talked a bit about it. He admitted that there was certainly a lot to be learned about how to run a hobby shop, and he was most uneasy about undertaking the venture, which showed considerable good judgment. It was very easy to counsel this young man, for he was realistic and understood the truth of what was being told to him, which was:

1. If he invested his $10,000 in a good education, no one could ever take it away from him. He would always have that education to rely upon, no matter what it was he wanted to do.

2. He knew nothing about the hobby shop business and was apt to lose his money rather rapidly, thus finding himself broke and with no education, a distressing thought.

3. He was young and was not sure that he would really like the hobby shop business once he got into it. He realized the difference between what something looked like from the outside and what it might be from the inside.

---

4. He recognized that he was not ready yet
    to settle down and work hard for a
    living. He wanted a few years to play a
    bit and develop.

He decided to go to college, which was what he wanted to do all along, except that his old man was trying to talk him out of it. Rarely do you encounter a situation where the kid is smarter than the old man, but it certainly seemed so in this instance.

Money spent on your formal education is an investment you make in yourself that can never be taken away from you. It only makes good sense to invest it wisely and get the most for your money. Indeed, one of the inside jokes in the academic world is, "A college education is one of the few things in the world a person pays money for and then walks off without."

If you are looking for a list of acceptable schools or some recommendations, you will not find one here. Such lists are asinine. Where you should go depends entirely upon what you want to do, where you live, your financial capabilities, your interests, your personality, and the situation of that school at that particular time.

A word needs to be said on that last point, for schools change with time. Indeed, a law of the academic world seems to be that the mighty shall fall and the meek shall rise. A certain school at one time may be at the pinnacle of academic esteem because of its programs and a few outstanding professors. Take note that the key to a school's excellence is in its faculty, not in its programs. It does not matter how fancy the program is or sounds; if the people who teach in it are not very good, the program will not be very good. When the faculty who has made a school famous moves on for any of several reasons, the excellence of that school is apt to change. Thus at any one time the schools offering the best training in a given field may differ considerably from the commonly accepted public ideas on the matter.

Experience

Previous mention has been made of the importance of the experience you gather during your career. A stint with certain companies tells knowledgeable people in the industry a great deal about the training and work habits that have been instilled in you. It is rather interesting to note the number of successful top executives in the publishing industry who started out as sales representatives with Prentice-Hall under the strict tutelage of Carl Hector. In contrast to other firms, Prentice-Hall not only gave its sales staff rigorous training, but also close supervision to ensure that they developed work habits productive to selling books. Unquestionably, people going through that program knew how to sell books, and knew what the publishing business was about. After all, if you were another publisher hiring a sales rep, wouldn't you like to know that the person you were hiring knew what the business was all about?

In the office equipment business IBM and Xerox are famous for their training programs. A person who has had a few years with IBM and has a successful record to show for it can easily find employment with a large number of other concerns, for potential employers recognize the excellence of the experience and the on-the-job training the individual has received.

A little story in regard to on-the-job training follows. Many years ago at the University of Colorado, Gary G. was an outstanding marketing major. He was president of the senior class, on the ski team, and so forth. He went to work for IBM and has had a most successful career. For two years after his graduation we laughed about the number of times we met on airplanes between San Francisco and Seattle. At that time I was going to both cities frequently, and it seemed that every time I crawled on an airplane in Denver there was Gary, heading either to San Jose or Seattle where IBM maintained training schools. He spent about half of his time in those early years participating in company training programs.

Do not underestimate the amount of education—yes, formal education—that can be yours if you go to work for certain companies. Other companies give you nothing; they hand you a briefcase, kick you out the door, and tell you to get 'em. Not a whole lot of good is likely to come from such situations.

Consequently, your decision about employers in your first few jobs is most important. Work for people who will develop you, from whom you can learn. Work for people who are recognized in the industry for developing good people. Get this experience on your record and it is yours forever. No one can take it away from you. It will travel with you to the grave.

It is time for another story to illustrate the importance of the experience you acquire. The point to this story is that there is a great deal of difference in the types of experiences you gain. It is one thing to be pushing a car over the road, setting up displays in retail stores day after day, week after week, but it is quite another thing to be exposed to a wide range of problems to be solved and things to be done.

A young man interested in retailing had offers from both Sears and Wards. He came into my office wanting to know which offer he should accept. Everyone had told him to go to work for Sears, for at that time (the mid-fifties) Wards was in terrible shape. In fact, at that time it was difficult to find many good reasons why someone would go to work for Wards, for certainly Sears was the darling of the merchandising world. However, I made this statement to the man: "Sears is certainly a top-notch company. If you go to work for Sears, you'll be made an assistant buyer in some division in some retail store and from there it will depend upon how good you are in relationship to all the other assistant buyers. Bear in mind that Sears has hired a lot of top-notch people. Most of the people with whom you'll be competing for promotion are good. I'm not saying that you won't be able to compete with them, for I know you're good. But the fact is that the competition for the top jobs will be fierce. Now let's take Wards. They haven't been able to hire very many people lately, yet they need them badly. You won't find the competition very keen. I would even go as far as to suggest that the door is wide open to the top, for someone has to do the job for them. The bank cashes their checks. I'm suggesting that your promotions and resultant pay may be brighter with Wards than with Sears. It would certainly seem that the experience you would gain by being in responsible positions would serve you well."

The man did not take too long to think it over. He accepted a job with Wards and was immediately, without training, made buyer for the camera department in the downtown Oklahoma City store. A few months later he was made manager of the Altus, Oklahoma store. In a few short months he had achieved a position that he might not ever have achieved with Sears. Moreover, no matter what happened to him afterward, he had on his record the experience of managing a store. Having such actual managerial experience is extremely valuable, for it tells potential employers a great deal that they want to know.

The moral of the story is that you must be careful not to assume that the company whose star is highest in the sky is automatically the best one to work for. Thousands of other people are going that route, which can make matters rather sticky. What you really should be looking for is an opportunity to gain much needed experience, and that opportunity may lie elsewhere. Here is another story on this point:

One day while attending a sales and marketing executives' convention in Kansas City, the personnel manager of a leading Kansas City department store was complaining about his inability to attract college graduates into their management training program. It so happened that I had taken three outstanding students with me to the luncheon and that they were sitting across from him. I looked at the man and said, "Well, here are three prospects for you. Start talking!"

It ended up that he hired one of them, Byron W., a most promising young man. Two months later Byron was back in the office. He had quit. I inquired why. "They stuck me in the shipping room and that was the last I saw of anyone. Just how long does it take to learn how to ship out packages? At the end of the third day I was bored stiff. Nobody said boo to me. I wasn't learning anything, so I quit."

The story does not end there. The store wanted him rather badly so they promised to mend their ways. He went back to work for them, this time as an assistant buyer in the toy department. A year later the story was the same. They had left him there and he was not learning anything; he was not gaining the experience he wanted.

He quit to work for the advertising department of General Electric, which, by the way, maintains a fine program for learning advertising. Byron was extremely happy with what he was learning at General Electric and became a valuable employee for them. It should not come as too much of a surprise to learn that the department store went out of business.

The moral of this story is that if you are a young person trying to develop and feel you are not getting the experience you need, if you are not learning something every day, if you are simply treading water, then you had best move on. Far too many people tread water all their lives, mired down in positions in which they cannot develop. If you do not develop in your early years, if you do not gain the experience you need to move on to higher echelons, if you allow yourself to get mired down in some routine job that stifles your development, you will find that time will rapidly pass you by until you are too old to move. Moreover, you may have lost the ability to develop.

Bear in mind that many employers have no desire whatsoever to develop you. They are perfectly happy to keep you in one job because you are doing it admirably well. They know that if you develop they may lose you. They cannot furnish what you want in the long run. The brutal truth is that your interests and those of your employer are in conflict. Your employer is concerned with his own best interests and you must be concerned with yours. The two are not necessarily the same.

Dan had earned his spurs in the Armstrong Cork training program, but because disenchanted with covering his assigned territory and began working for a large lumber company in Denver as an inside seller. An inside seller sits at a desk all day taking orders over the telephone. It was an important job in the lumber company, for a good telephone seller can do a great deal to increase sales by reminding the buyer of some needs. It takes someone of intelligence, for one must be able to quote prices rapidly and to recall quickly the availability of materials.

Dan was magnificent at the job, but he had taken it only temporarily with the understanding that the firm would give him a territory when one opened up. He wanted outside selling. However, the longer Dan was at the telephone, the more valuable he became to the company. Each time he asked his boss to put him into a territory the response would be a raise and a conversation about how good he was at his job. The trouble was that Dan was not developing. He finally saw that he could spend the rest of his life on the telephone. The longer he was on that contraption the more valuable he was to the company but the less good he was doing himself. One day he resigned when he finally concluded that he was committing career suicide. He took a job that led into sales management, where he wanted to be.

WHAT DO YOU WANT YOUR EXPERIENCE RECORD TO LOOK LIKE?

Visualize for a moment your experience written down on your resume, for, after all, that is what employers are going to see. First, they like to see companies whose names they recognize. When they see that you have worked for some leading concern such as IBM, Xerox, Procter & Gamble, Armstrong Cork, Burlington Industries, Levi Strauss, Florsheim Shoe, General Electric, U.S. Steel, or Frito-Lay, they have some idea of what you have learned. If they see that you have worked for Universal Widget, they do not have the faintest idea of what you did or what you know, thus the burden of proving the merit of your experience with Universal Widget rests upon you. There is some merit in working for recognized concerns.

What you did with those concerns is of importance. What was the job you held with the company? A case could be made that it would be far better to be a sales manager of a small concern than a sales representative for Procter & Gamble; you had the opportunity to have learned more with the smaller firm. Thus, your job title and what you did with your employer may be more important than the company for whom you were working.

Bear in mind the attitude of a potential boss. He wants to know what you can do for him. To make that judgment, he wants to know what you have done for other people. If you have done something for someone else that he wants you to do for him, then he feels comfortable because you have already been doing the job successfully.

This brings us to another important aspect: how well you did on the job. Potential employers want to see a history of success, one in which you start with an employer to do a job and you do it successfully. And what evidence do they use to judge your success on the job? Several things.

First, were you promoted? It is normally assumed that if you are successful at one thing, you will be promoted to do something else. The person who worked for five years at one task and was not promoted is certainly looked upon with great suspicion, and justifiably so. After all, here is a person working closely with a supervisor over a period of years and that supervisor has never deemed a promotion proper. Moreover, the person has never felt sufficiently put upon to quit the job, so evidently, must have felt fairly evaluated—not a pretty set of thoughts, but accurate. Talented people simply do not sit still in a lowly job for five years without being promoted or having some other rewards to show for their performance.

Second, your pay raises are part of your history that will be examined. Good performance is normally rewarded with pay raises. If you show substantial financial progress, that is solid evidence of your worth.

Third, tangible proof of your accomplishments is persuasive. Visualize your impact on a potential employer if you are able to say, "I took over the New England territory and increased its sales from $200,000 to $400,000 the first year," or "I developed an advertising program for the new widget." It is important to be able to point to something you did, something you accomplished that was successful. Whenever possible you should have proof of your accomplishments with you in whatever form they may be.

Continual Education

It is important to understand that you will never be through with education. Look at the medical and legal professions. Doctors and lawyers continually attend clinics and programs to keep them up to date. Not only have you a great deal to learn to bring you up to proficiency, but you must continue to learn to keep up with all the changes. Thousands of programs proliferate in the American business scene. Granted, many are worthless or mediocre, still many others are worthwhile and accomplish their objectives. Also, bear in mind that a program worthless to you may be of benefit to someone else.

Perhaps the Dale Carnegie programs are a case in point. People have attended Dale Carnegie programs who feel that they did not get their money's worth; however, many more feel it was most worthwhile. The person who has trouble meeting and speaking with people certainly needs help in those areas, and programs such as the one offered by Dale Carnegie can be of assistance.

One cannot take programs indiscriminately, for many frauds are on the market. Programs sell for thousands of dollars proclaiming to do great things for you, but they fall far short of the mark. Thus, you need to take heed and carefully evaluate not only the intrinsic merit of such programs but also your own need for what they purport to do. A program may be ill-advised for you and may still have merit for someone else because of the person's particular deficiencies. Perhaps the best source of information for evaluating the merits of such educational programs would be persons who have taken the program. Find out what the program's former customers say about it.

The cost of many of these programs may be borne either entirely or partially by one's employer. Moreover, many bosses look with favor upon someone who spends time—preferably one's own time—getting such training. One young career in a good-sized manufacturing company was nipped in the bud by the young woman's refusal to attend training sessions on her own time. She maintained, "The company wants me to go to these programs, so let them give me the time off to do it. My time off is my own to do with as I want. They don't own me!" Noble sentiments, perhaps, but not conducive to building a career, for her boss said, "If I'm willing to foot the bill for the program, then she ought to be willing to spend her own time. After all, she's the one who benefits from the training in the long run. Since she's not willing to spend her time for her own development, then forget it."

SOURCES OF PROGRAMS

Considering the numerous types of programs available, let's take a brief look—but certainly not a comprehensive one—at some of the more common types of programs.

Trade Associations Every industry has one or more trade associations. One common function of such organizations is to provide the people in the industry with needed educational programs. Many of these programs are held in connection with conventions and meetings. However, you should not rely too much upon this source for your development because the efforts of trade associations at this date along these lines have not been impressive. Take what you can from them, but do not expect too much. (At the present time, the author is developing a series of programs for the Menswear Retailers of America (MRA) that are designed to help develop the skills of budding merchants.)

Professional Associations More important in the American industrial structure is the role of the professional association—the American Medical Association, American Bar Association, American Management Association, Sales and Marketing Executives, Purchasing Agent, the engineering societies, the Society of Certified Public Accountants, and so on. Each professional association normally has a rather impressive program of educational activities. Usually the quality of these programs is good and your attendance at these programs can be most beneficial to you. By all means you should consider it part of your personal development to join and actively participate in these professional associations. They can play an important role in your professional development.

Universities Many of our nation's leading universities conduct postgraduate or executive development programs of varying natures. While some of the more famous executive development programs are designed to perfect your total performance as a business executive, many special purpose programs are designed to perfect some specific skill. USC held one on the copyright laws as they pertain to literary creations that was well attended by lawyers and agents who deal in the publishing and entertainment businesses. Similarly, many universities conduct programs for certain other industries. USC does a considerable amount of work for the foodservice industry through its food distribution center. Cornell, Michigan State, and Denver do a great deal for the hotel and restaurant business through their institutes for the foodservice industry. SMU continually offers a large number of courses and institutes to help small businessmen better manage their affairs. In 1980 The SMU Cox School of Business will offer over 200 two- and three-day sessions on all aspects of business.

Profit-making Enterprises Many educational programs have been developed by profit-making enterprises, such as Dale Carnegie, Xerox, Success Motivation Institute, and American Management Association, who are in the business of selling education. These programs can be rather expensive. Their merit depends entirely upon the particular program and your sophistication in the subject matter. It is not exactly fair for an experienced sales representative to take a beginning salesmanship course and then complain that it is too elementary. The key questions are whether the program is designed for you and whether you are capable of absorbing it at your present stage of development.

A word about this latter point: some individuals have been turned off by university executive development programs that stress top management decision making and business policy. The root of their dissatisfaction was not that the subject matter was unworthy, but rather that they simply lacked the background and sophistication to really appreciate what business policy is about.

Reading Programs

Perhaps more important than your continuing educational programs is the matter of your regular reading habits. What magazines and books do you read? You can learn a great deal (if not most) of what you need to know through self-study if you have the mental discipline to do so. Thousands of books are published each year on every useful subject imaginable. Magazines and periodicals pertinent to your field no doubt flourish by the dozens. You need to develop an orderly program for absorbing these materials. If you are in business, you should be reading *Business Week* and *Forbes* regularly. Perhaps you would get a lot out of *The Wall Street Journal* and *Fortune*. Try a few issues to see. And then there are the many professional journals in each of the fields; you will have to judge for yourself whether or not they are worth your time.

People in the technical fields have an even larger problem keeping abreast of available information, for many more professional journals are published in these areas. It is impossible here to give a list of publications for each profession, for the numbers are staggering. Reading the publications concerned with your industry is particularly important, for someone who fails to keep up with what is going on in one's industry is not apt to impress many people.

BOOKS

Books can be rather frustrating. The fact that you are reading this book is evidence that you recognize information can be obtained from books. However, many people have expectations that are far too high. Quite honestly, this author has purchased many books, perused them, and thrown them in the wastebasket with the comment that the work was useless. The book contained nothing for me. However, there was no regret over spending the money on that book; it would be unreasonable to expect to find some great truth in every book. That just is not going to happen. Indeed, some books are infuriating because not only are they without value for me, but I feel they are putting forth much misinformation. But these are personal values others do not share. That is freedom of the press.

One top sales executive put it a nice way. "I buy every book published in my field. Most of the time there is nothing new in a book, but I never regret reading it because the review alone helps me out. I have yet to read a book that did not force me to recall something important I had forgotten. Moreover, if I get just one idea from a book— that's all I'm looking for, just one—then the price of that book is small compared to the rewards that I will get with that idea."

Perhaps that sales executive's philosophy will help you reconcile your attitude toward many books. Just bear in mind that if you get one helpful idea, you have your money's worth. Every sentence in a book does not have to be pure gold for you to benefit from it. Moreover, remember that there is considerable educational merit in reading things with which you disagree or which may be totally in error if, by such reading, you are forced into developing counterarguments and forced to think about the proposition at hand. You do not have to agree with everything you read in order for it to help you develop.

While it may seem self-serving to many people for an author to stress the importance of reading books, still I feel so strongly about this matter from personal observation that I must comment on it. I have yet to meet a business leader who was not an avid reader. These people read just about everything, from the newspaper to the encyclopedia. They are hungry for information. They want to know what is going on in the world, what people are doing in other industries and in other companies. When so many business leaders and successful people read extensively, it is difficult to ignore the importance of reading.

The Development of Administrative Skills

One member of the Young Presidents' Organization (YPO), when questioned about how he developed his administrative skills, advanced this idea. "After I got out of college and settled down into my first job, I made a point to get involved in all sorts of community activities, any group that would take me. Little League, church, neighborhood, you name it and I joined it. I volunteered to do whatever had to be done. I found out that you can learn a great deal about how to get people to do what you want them to do—managing them, if you will—in just such activities. At first I found I was terrible at it. I remember the first year was awful. Everything was messed up, nothing flowed right, and I couldn't organize my people. I didn't do a very good job of it, but with experience I learned the ropes. I learned how to organize projects, how to line up things, and how to get things done. I attribute a large part of my success in business to those early years in community activities where I learned to manage people."

That is the way one person developed administrative skills. He learned by projecting himself into situations requiring administrative skills and then was perceptive enough to learn them. Let's see what another individual, the vice-president of manufacturing for a large machine tool company, did to develop administrative skills. "In my first years with the company I seized every opportunity I could to show some management skills. I remember that first year the boss wanted someone to organize the company picnic. I stepped forward and knocked myself out to make sure that was the best run picnic the company ever had. And it was! The boss never forgot that. For the next ten years he was continually reminding me of the great job I did on that picnic. Then there was the time we had all of the confusion when the workers struck. We were trying to keep the plant open to get out critical orders and run the place on a skeleton staff. I worked 'round the clock organizing that effort and I think more than anything else that was responsible for getting me where I am now. The boss was really impressed with how I held things together during that strike."

A sales manager relates, "I always wanted to be in sales management and I spent a lot of time thinking about how I was ever going to prove to Mr. Howard (the boss) that I had management skills. One day he hired a new salesman and I saw an opportunity. I walked into his office and volunteered to help train the new man. He was so happy to get rid of the responsibility that he agreed. I really trained that young man and he was immediately successful in the field. Time after time Mr. Howard would comment about how much he liked my ability to train new salespeople. I think that was responsible for my promotions."

The moral of these stories seems clear: you must aggressively seize every opportunity to use administrative skills. You will only develop these talents if you use them. You will never be a manager if you simply go along your merry way ducking responsibility for making things happen.

PERCEPTIVE OBSERVATION OF ADMINISTRATIVE TACTICS

The world of administration is largely unseen. The acts and thinking behind administrative affairs go largely unreported in the trade press and in books. Some administrative skills can be learned by carefully observing how good administrators do their jobs and what makes poor administrators failures. While there is much to be learned from observation, the problem is that most people are not attuned to perceiving what is really going on in some matter from an administrative context. When the boss does not say anything or do anything that makes sense, the average person is likely to suppose that the boss is simply off the ball. It never occurs to the person that perhaps such behavior might be a deliberate administrative tactic.

Consider the individual who has been passed over on pay and promotions and who roundly condemns his superiors as a bunch of blockheads for their inability to see his finer virtues and reward him commensurately.

The reality of the situation may be that the yokel is being fired and is too stupid to know it, that it is a deliberate administrative tactic. Or take the individual who complains that he (or she) is not part of the work group, that people are ignoring him, and that he is given no responsibility. Seldom does he perceive all these things as deliberate administrative tactics designed to force him out. He has not been given any responsibilities because management does not feel he is capable of executing them.

Make no mistake about it, your success or failure as an administrator is determined largely by how adept you are at tactical maneuvering. Most of the people who lose their jobs as administrators do not do so because of the lack of technical proficiency. Rather, it is because of their use of improper tactics.

Let's take the career of one most promising man who had made it to the top in an enterprise, only to be forced to resign by a conspiracy among the senior people of his organization. The man had instituted many programs that everyone admitted were quite worthy. He also had a great charm and considerable intelligence. Nevertheless, his career is in shambles today because he neglected to learn a few basic administrative tactics. In this case, upon assuming command of the organization he failed to establish communications with his senior people to build a foundation on which to work with them. He treated them with disdain and largely ignored them while he pursued essential activities in the marketplace—getting new customers. The senior people conspired and approached the board of directors with their list of grievances (there is usually such a list). The chairman asked for the man's resignation.

He had made three mistakes. The first was his failure to establish relationships with those senior people and the second was that he was absent from the battlefield so much that he really did not know what was going on. The conspiracy had succeeded before he even knew it was taking place. Finally, he had committed a classic blunder: he formed his own hanging committee. He had appointed a group of these same senior people to a committee to study the reorganization of the company. Their sole recommendation for reorganization was that he should be fired. Now that was an inept administrator!

The moral of the story is that while you may think such an illustration is a rare item, it is not. Administrative happenings occur around you all the time. Every time someone gets hired or fired a story is behind it. Study people and what they do, then look at their results and judge accordingly. When you see someone who has successfully been able to maintain a position at the top, then you should study that person rather carefully to see what allows him to remain there. When you see someone who has failed, try to pinpoint the reasons for the failure and go forth a bit wiser.

Emotional Development

Several books claim that most of us remain children much of our lives. Most people are rather immature in their behavior and attitudes, and these immaturities block their personal development. One of the key things sought in appraising someone for promotion is that person's emotional maturity. A child is not likely to be promoted into a position of responsibility, yet many grown men and women act like children most of their lives and wonder why they do not go very far. Some examples:

A salesman stomps into his manager's office with a grievance. "Jill's got a parking place right next to the building and I have to park down with the workers. I want a parking place beside Jill." This sounds like a little kid— Johnny's got a new toy and I want one, too! Now the sales manager has a lot more to worry about than where this guy parks his car, so he is not apt to be too sympathetic with this crybaby. Moreover, the truly perceptive manager knows well that if this man wanted a better parking place there are certainly better tactics to use than the one he is using. The clever person would find a way to get a parking place without appearing to be a crybaby. Thus the salesman is marked as immature and inept.

Ask any university dean about the emotional maturity of most of his professors and he will shake his head in wonderment. The stories they tell! One professor told his dean, "I don't really care how much of a raise you give me this year, so long as it's more than so-and-so's." Another said, "I've got fifty kids in my class and so-and-so only has thirty-five. That's not fair!" The whining goes on and on about office space, lighting, parking, you name it. These people seldom get managerial jobs because they do not have the emotional maturity to be good managers.

Now how do you go about developing this emotional maturity? That is another matter, not an easy one to discuss, for it requires a great deal of wisdom and perspective. Several fundamental reasons exist for the types of emotional immaturities described. First, there is the matter of egotism. Some people are so egocentric that they do not care about anyone else's problems. The person demands better parking space. All he knows is that he is unhappy with where he is parking. He does not really care about anything else—that there are no better parking places open, that the administrator has a hundred other people with more seniority and rank entitled to better places is beside the point to this disgruntled employee. All he knows is that his wishes are not being satisfied, so he will throw a tantrum. This is a childish and immature action. Emotional maturity demands that the individual see and understand his proper place in the total picture and that he recognize the rights of others and not think that the world will rearrange itself for his convenience.

Second, the immature mind simply does not understand the complexity of things. Things are never as simple as they seem. The clerk in the department store is disgustedly complaining about all of the paperwork. The clerk rants and raves to anyone who will listen (and not many people will, for long) about how the system should be changed here and there. Well, the mature individual knows how difficult it is to change any system, even small ones, let alone large ones. The mature person tries to understand the whole problem and does not go around popping off about something to people with no real solution.

Mature people have control over their emotions and do not panic under stress. Managers operate under conditions that place great stress on them, yet if they lose control of their emotions they will be ineffective. Emotions block good judgment. Decisions made while emotionally disturbed are not apt to be wise ones; thus a cool head is an administrative asset.

The Resume

Much has been written in books and periodicals about how to prepare an effective resume. This is not the place to delve into the technical details of resume formats. Other books deal with that important topic in great detail. Rather, let us consider some philosophy that may be at odds with what you may have read elsewhere. Hasten not to the conclusion that you are urged to accept these thoughts in preference to those of others, but rather to think of them as alternatives for your consideration. The decisions about your resume are yours to make.

A lot of nonsense has been written about resumes. I harbor this belief both from the point of view of an administrator looking at thousands of resumes while hiring people and from the point of view of a job applicant. My experience has been distinctly in contrast to many of the recommendations made by many resume experts.

LENGTH OF RESUME

Many experts insist that a resume must be short and hard-hitting. They insist that it should be only one page, that unless you grab the reader's attention in one page you will not likely get it. Perhaps, but I think not. If all you have to offer an employer can be put on one page, then you do not have much to sell. If you have the background and experience that the employer is looking for to fill an important job, rest assured that he will read whatever you put in his hands, as long as it is *relevant* and *interesting*. You really need not concern yourself with length. Length takes care of itself. As long as what you say is relevant and interesting to the reader it will be read, whether it is one page, three pages, or twenty pages. The hiring executive realizes that he has nothing more important to do than hiring the right person for the vacant position. I assume that you are going for a position of some importance. Since that position is important, the employer wants to know everything relevant about the applicant.

I do not know how many hundreds of one- and two-page resumes I have dumped in the "out" basket with the notation to my secretary to send them the standard rejection letter simply because the resumes told little about the people, merely some glib generalities that did nothing to differentiate them from the hundreds of other applicants. *The resume must get the reader's attention.* It must demand to be read.

I distinctly remember an eight-page resume packaged nicely in an attractive, folded form that was so outstanding that I decided to make a special effort to meet the person, even though he did not have the qualifications we needed. I only wanted to make his acquaintance, for his resume was so outstanding that I assure you I read every word of it. Again, the key is that the resume was interesting and relevant.

Granted, the reader has no desire to read page after page of your experiences in the Scouts or in the church group at age thirteen. If you want to build your resume with that type of material, then you had best keep it brief.

TWO TYPES OF RESUMES

The length of the resume really depends upon the type of resume you are creating. One is the general, all-purpose resume handed out willy-nilly to anyone. It is usually two or three pages at best, perhaps longer if you have had extensive experience. This one you keep in your file, ready for use at any time.

Then there is the resume you put together for specifically applying for a given job. This resume is sometimes called a *portfolio* and you can include anything you think will help you get the job. Perhaps you include transcripts of your college work; perhaps you include samples of your previous work. Such resumes may run seven or eight pages, depending upon one's work experience and how much one has to tell.

The all-time high in resume preparation, at least to my knowledge, was furnished by Russ Potts, the SMU athletic director. Three days after it was announced that the former athletic director had resigned, each member of the SMU athletic committee received a fifty-six-page, yes that's right, *fifty-six-page* resume bound in blue leather with the words, "A Return to Glory" emblazoned on this in red. (SMU colors are blue and red.) Inside those covers was a tremendously impressive presentation of what Russ had done and what he proposed to do. He got the job. I later learned that two months prior to the former athletic director's resignation, Russ had his assistant come to Dallas and make a thorough study of the SMU situation. Evidently he had anticipated the resignation and wanted the job. More importantly, he has more than lived up to his promises.

One advantage of the longer portfolio is that is saves a great deal of time during personal interviews. The person you are talking with has had a chance to read about you and is thus relieved of the need to inquire about many of the routine facts about you. You can get right into the heart of an interview and skip the usual preludes.

Next, you can really do the job of proving your capabilities—what you have done and what you can do. Bill Bergman, the young man featured in the resumes shown in Figures 2 and 3 (see the end of Part 1), was asked by Grey Advertising to prepare a portfolio of his work for their consideration. In it he was asked to develop some advertisements for three hypothetical products, thus giving him the chance to prove his capabilities.

PROVE YOUR ABILITIES

Once you have gained some business experience employers are most interested in your job histories. What do you know? What have you done? What can you do? What success have you had on the job? What accomplishments can you claim? All of these experiences can be gone into in detail in your resume. Tell people what you have done. Tell them about your experiences. Be prepared to prove your abilities. Try to convey the idea in your resume that you are someone who gets the job done, who is successful, and who is a winner.

INTERESTING

An employer may receive hundreds of resumes for one position, and the pity of it is, ninety-nine out of a hundred of them look the same. The employer cannot remember one from another. While many experts object to the following advice, still it may be valid in many circumstances. Find a way to make your resume different from the others, something that makes the employer remember it. Perhaps color will do the job. Perhaps format will do it. Whatever, make an impression! Make your resume interesting! You want to stimulate its reader to the point where he is thinking, "I've got to see this person. I'd better talk with him. He sounds interesting."

WHAT CAN YOU DO FOR THE EMPLOYER?

The employer wants to know what you can do for him (or her). How are you prepared to make money for the firm? You must manage to put in an inkling of this information. Some resumes come out blatantly with a section entitled,

"What I Can Do For You," or "Why You Should Hire Me." One unemployed materials systems manager titled a resume section, "Here's How I Can Make You More Money." Many people feel such sections are in bad taste since they are rather brassy. However, consider for a moment that if you cannot blow your own horn a bit in your resume, just who is going to do it for you? You are not a movie star with an agent selling your skills to the buyer. You have to sell yourself. Moreover, many business executives wonder why they should hire somebody to help sell their company if the individual cannot sell himself properly. So do not worry about being too brassy, although admittedly it is possible to come on too strong. Much depends upon the personality of the intended reader and the job in question. Someone seeking a job in sales or marketing is expected to be bolder than someone applying for a job as a trust officer in a bank. You need to appraise the personality of your intended target reader. Your resume can be more effective if you have obtained some information about this person. If you can, tailor your resume to the likings of the person you are trying to impress.

THE PROFESSIONAL RESUME

Hundreds of firms are in the business of helping people develop their resumes. I had the painful experience of observing a friend pay a goodly sum of money to avail himself of the service of one such nationally famous organization. The price was $4,500—or would the term "rip-off" be more appropriate? This organization belonged to the one-sheet-resume cult. They developed a polished, smooth, jazzy, one-sheet resume proclaiming my friend to be a top corporate financial officer. I did not get a look at this $4,500 resume until several months later after he had no success in getting even a nibble through this organization's efforts. They had sent out thousands of these one-sheet resumes and had not even received bite number one. Imagine that! Thousands of resumes had gone out to all the leading corporations in the country, and there was not one single response. When I answered a late night rapping at my door, I discovered my friend. After two hours of aimless chit-chat and a few martinis, he finally got around to the point of the visit. He was at the end of his rope. He had had no success getting a job, and he wanted me to look over his whole program, particularly his resume. I asked him if he had it with him. He pulled it out and that is when I saw the one-page fraud. I could not believe my eyes. That resume said absolutely nothing! No wonder he did not get any response to it—it was nothing but hot air. There was not one hard fact in it. I do not know why anybody would ever think that a responsible executive would be receptive to anything like that. Oh, yeah ... it was jazzy, but it was written to make the job seeker feel good. The resume was composed of glowing terms describing how great he was. It was nothing but hogwash designed to inflate the job applicant's ego; it was not designed to get him a job.

Well, we wrote out a different resume, one that had some facts in it, and two weeks later he had a job as vice-president of a leading national organization. He had good capabilities, but you certainly would not know it from that terrible thing that outfit had written for him. So much for the professional resume writer. I personally do not think they are worth a damn, but if you have that type of money to throw away on your ego, fine. It's your dough.

SAMPLE RESUMES

A traditional resume is shown in Figure 1. Just to give you an idea of what an imaginative resume looks like, Bill Bergman's is shown in Figures 2 and 3.

KEEP AN UP-TO-DATE RESUME HANDY AT ALL TIMES

How one seldom knows when one is going to need a resume has always amazed me. I have encountered situations where a resume has been demanded on five minutes' notice. Had I not had one handy, I might have lost a particularly lucrative job. You should always have your resume up-to-date and ready for distribution. You seldom know when it will be needed. Do you have one now? If you don't... get with it!

WILLIAM P. GARRISON   5444 South Woodside Avenue   Tel. (312) 567-6969
                             Chicago, Illinois 60653

job objective

To begin work in office of Comptroller or Treasurer of small manufacturing organization located in Midwest, preferably near Chicago, with purpose of qualifying
eventually for general management responsibilities.

education   GRADUATE SCHOOL OF BUSINESS   UNIVERSITY OF CHICAGO

1973 to present

Candidate for degree of Master of Business Administration in June 1975. Concen-
trating in finance with strong preparation in accounting and economics. Dean's
List during first three quarters. Member of Business Club. Number Two man on
University Tennis Team. Expenses financed through Sears Roebuck Foundation and
Fellowship.

1964 to 1968

Received A. B. degree, cum laude, in June 1968. Majored in English with three
courses in economics, including industrial organization and public policy.
President of Delta Kappa Epsilon, social fraternity. Member of Glee Club.
Captain of Tennis team in senior year. Played intramural football. Expenses
financed partially through scholarship, summer jobs and part-time work as waiter
in college dining halls.

experience   JAMES P. OSGOOD AND COMPANY   NEW YORK CITY

Securities and Commodities Brokers, investment bankers with thirteen branch sales
offices in East and Midwest. Member of New York Stock Exchange and other exchanges.

1971 to 1973

After training, assigned as securities analyst, reporting to the Director of
Research. Duties involved analyzing current stock issues and industry trends.
Assisted in preparing weekly market letter made available to customers. Wrote
reports on specific stocks or situations as requested by partners. Qualified by
New York Stock Exchange as registered representative. Resigned in September 1973
to attend Graduate School of Business.

Summer work held during college years included camp counselor, construction
laborer and carpenter's helper.

Military service - U. S. Navy - Upon graduation from college, entered Naval
Officer Candidate School, Newport, Rhode Island. After completing four-month
program, commissioned as Ensign and assigned to U. S. S. Vulcan. Duties ranged
from Assistant Gunnery Officer, responsible for operation of ship's radar.
Received commendation for research in preparing Air Defense Manual. Released
from active duty in June 1971.

Activities. Interested in classical music. Member of Downtown Choral Society
while in New York. Enjoy sailing and skiing when time permits. Active in
high school athletics. Elected class president in senior year.

References. Will be furnished upon request.

Planning   73

If I Had Gone to NYU or Columbia, We'd Have Already Met.

But since I'm going to graduate school in the southwest, it's not that easy for us to get together. So let me take a few minutes to introduce myself.

My name is Bill Bergman and this August I'll graduate from SMU with a Masters of Business Administration.

As a career goal, I want to work on an account team of a large advertising agency.

Now for a 22-year old, attaining a goal like that isn't easy. It takes years of busting your brains in the library, gaining practical experience, and developing the discipline to work 25 hours a day.

Sure. Advertising is tough to break into. But if you've been trained like I have, meeting the competition head on is what makes the business so exciting.

Undergraduate Education

In May of 1974, I graduated from the University of Oklahoma with a bachelors degree in advertising through the school of journalism.

As a junior, I won the Leslie Rice Memorial Award in Advertising. And as a senior, I was elected into Kappa Tau Alpha, the national journalism scholarship society.

My activities as an undergraduate included three years on the campus newspaper where I served as wire editor, staff writer, and columnist.

I was president of the Stewart Harrell chapter of the Public Relations Student Society of America and managing editor of their national publication, the Forum.

As a member of the OU debate team, I participated in intercollegiate debate tournaments on such topics as national health care.

During my junior year, I was a resident advisor in a freshman dormitory of 60 screaming maniacs.

Finally, I was a pledge trainer of the Alpha Epsilon Pi social fraternity.

Work Experience

Presently, I'm doing an internship with Glenn, Bozell & Jacobs here in Dallas. Working with the account team in charge of packaged goods, I've done everything from writing client contact reports to aiding in development of marketing plans.

Last summer, I worked at Tempo Advertising in New Orleans, my hometown. There, I served as an assistant account executive working on several accounts including an amusement park and a local rootbeer bottler.

Late in the summer, I was employed by Crain Publications as a student assistant to their annual *Advertising Age* Creative Workshop in New York.

My first taste of the agency business came in the summer of 1972 when I was an office boy at Peter Mayer Advertising.

The next summer I returned to that agency, this time in the account services department doing marketing research for the agency's biggest client, Wembley Ties.

A Determined MBA

I've been working too hard and too long to let a couple of hundred miles get in my way.

More than anything, I want to go into the agency business. And I've got the motivation, maturity, and education to prove it.

If you'd like to meet me or have some references sent, write me at my school address:

5200 Belmont
Apt. 220
Dallas, Texas 75206
(214) 824-3983

or at my permanent home address:

2114 Jefferson Ave.
New Orleans, Louisiana 70115
(504) 891-6531

SOUTHERN METHODIST UNIVERSITY

Figure 2

When you're 21 and fresh out of college you gotta be willing to work your tail off to be good.

Whiz kids aren't born overnight. It's 28-hour days, sleepless nights and a real love for advertising that has made them successful.

Sure. It's easy to say that you like advertising. But to sincerely love the business you've got to enjoy the tension, the pressure and the millions of headaches that accompany fierce competition.

My name is Bill Bergman and this May I'll be graduating from the University of Oklahoma with a degree in advertising and marketing.

In four years of college I didn't achieve academic success through luck. It was hard work and a real love for what I was studying that has allowed me to maintain a 3.6 overall grade average.

Grades alone though are only an indicator of one's ability. So let me tell you a little bit more about what I've done in the past four years.

Work Experience

I've had quite a bit of experience in journalism and advertising in school as well as in the summers.

For two summers now I've worked at Peter Mayer Advertising in New Orleans, my hometown.

The first summer I was an office boy.

The next summer, though, I worked in the account services department doing marketing research for the agency's biggest client, Wembley Ties. Also, I assisted account executives on many of the agency's retail accounts.

Here at school I've been business manager of the yearbook. Managing editor of the *Forum* which is a national publication of the Public Relations Student Society of America. And I've been a staff writer, wire editor and most recently a columnist on the campus newspaper, the *Oklahoma Daily*.

Finally, last year I was a counselor in the dorms planning activities and helping 62 residents cope with the problems of college life.

Major Campus Activities

As president of the Stewart Harrell chapter of the Public Relations Student Society of America, I have helped in bringing speakers to campus as well as organizing promotional campaigns for student organizations.

As a member of the debate team, I've participated in intercollegiate debate tournaments on such topics as national health care.

When I was pledge trainer of the Alpha Epsilon Pi social fraternity, I spent many sleepless nights helping freshmen face the problems of adjusting to a new way of life.

In an advertising campaigns class, I served as president and creative director of a student ad agency that was in competition with three other agencies all pitching for the same account. My agency won by a unanimous vote of the journalism and marketing faculty, and a group of advertising professionals.

And as a member of the University of Oklahoma Speakers Forum, I was a major speaker on the topic of Women's Liberation.

References

Selling myself, my ideas and my organizations is what has made my college years so successful.

Guiding and teaching me through these years have been three people. They are:

Peter A. Mayer, President
Peter Mayer Advertising, Inc.
816 Howard Ave.
New Orleans, Louisiana 70113

Nora Owens, Vice President
Lowe Runkle Company
1800 Liberty Tower
Oklahoma City, Oklahoma 73102

Frank Heaston
Professor of Advertising
(15 years with Gardner Advertising)
Copeland Hall
860 Van Fleet Oval
Norman, Oklahoma 73069

Why hire Bill Bergman?

Youth. Aggressiveness. And a strong desire to learn is what I have to offer.

I'll work my tail off because it's hard work and a sincere love for what you're doing that makes advertising such an exciting business.

If you're interested and you'd like to meet me at my school address:

1705 E. Lindsey
Apt. 2
Norman, Oklahoma 73069
(405) 329-1519

or at my permanent home address:

2114 Jefferson Ave.
New Orleans, Louisiana 70115
(504) 891-6531

Figure 3

PART 2

On the Job

Your First Job

Your first significant job on your chosen career path is especially important for several reasons. You should give it considerable thought and exert an unusually large amount of effort in getting started properly.

Now do not jump to the conclusion that if you don't get the right first job all is lost, because that would be obvious nonsense. Many people start out in unfortunate positions and recover quite nicely. All we are saying is that getting off to a good start gives you a lead in the race for the top. Having the right first job is simply an advantage you can have if you are able to pull it off.

What Your First Job Should Do For You

You should obtain five things from your first position: training, experience, credentials, exposure, and contacts.

TRAINING

Perhaps the most important thing your first job can do is to give you the training you need to proceed in your chosen profession. Indeed, many people deliberately seek employment with certain firms famous for their training programs. The reputations of IBM, Xerox, Procter & Gamble, Armstrong Cork, and other such firms is so well established that many people choose to spend a bit of time with those concerns simply to gain their training. You know you need the training, so it makes all the sense in the world to go to someone who will give it to you. The value of such training far exceeds any differentials in pay, so you should not give a second thought to accepting a lower wage from a company that will give you excellent training.

EXPERIENCE

Obviously, your first job will give you your first real feel of experience. However, there are experiences and there are experiences. With some companies the experience you gain will be routine and have a very narrow base. In short, you will not grow with such companies, for you are not getting the wide range of meaningful experiences to develop your talent. Other companies will thrust you into situations where the experiences you gain will be both meaningful and helpful to your future.

Joe M. had an offer from one of the large soap companies and also one from a small shutter manufacturer. He currently foresaw that if he went to work for the soap company his experience would be largely limited to selling soap products in supermarkets—fighting for display space and helping the retailer merchandise the company's products. However, with the shutter manufacturer Joe correctly guessed that he would be getting into not only all phases of marketing but also many other phases of running small businesses. Since he eventually wanted to be in business for himself, he accepted the job with the shutter manufacturer; he felt that the experience would be much more relevant to his career goals. His actual experience on the job proved he was correct, for in a few short years he gained the broad experiences he needed to establish his own concern.

Care should be taken to examine carefully the promises some employers make about providing you with a range of experiences and their actual performance. Try to talk to some people who have gone down the same path previously.

CREDENTIALS

In certain fields it is important that you gain credentials. It is one thing to have on your resume that you worked for Clot's Department Store, but quite another to be able to say that you worked for Neiman-Marcus or Bergdorf-Goodman. People who have worked for certain well-recognized firms gain a certain status in the eyes of other people. It is assumed when you work for certain individuals that you must not only be highly talented (why else would these esteemed employers have hired you?), but also that you had to gain a great deal of valuable experience from them. Mary K. accepted employment at Neiman-Marcus at a salary well below what she could have received elsewhere. Mary wanted to be a fashion merchandiser, a buyer of high-fashion goods for department stores. She accepted the job with Neiman-Marcus largely because of the credentials it would give her in obtaining employment elsewhere. She felt the training programs and experience she could have gained by starting with other department stores would be better than that available from Neiman's; nevertheless, she wanted the Neiman-Marcus credentials. She has gone on to much better positions and has never regretted her decision.

EXPOSURE

Elsewhere in this book the theory of exposure has been expounded. It is important for your career that you be exposed to all sorts of people and situations in business. If you are buried in the back room of some concern, seldom seeing anyone, your exposure is definitely limited; you are not apt to be very worldly about what is going on around you nor will other people ever come to know you.

You will be much as the desert flower destined to bloom and die largely unseen by others.

Some jobs provide far more exposure than others. One young woman decided to accept employment with Xerox in order to execute a certain strategy. She knew she wanted a position somewhere in general management with a medium-sized manufacturing concern. She felt that by selling Xerox copying machines she would automatically have entree into all the manufacturing concerns in her city, plus come to know the people in them and their situations. More importantly, she would know whether or not they had use for her services. She felt the Xerox job gave her maximum exposure in her community.

CONTACTS

Closely akin to exposure is the matter of contacts. However, the two differ in such significant ways that they should be mentioned separately. One can have a great deal of exposure, yet make few meaningful contacts. A contact is an acquaintanceship with some individual in a position to help your career.

CONCLUSION

Thus, when considering a first job, you should carefully determine just what that job is going to do for you. Look for some assurance that it will lead in the direction you wish to go.

Warning: Do not misconstrue the intent of this section, for just about any job may be better than no job at all. It is quite possible for a person to become so particular and demanding that he is unable to find a job meeting all his specifications. It is far more important to work and learn something, for a great deal can be learned on any job, than it is to sit around waiting for just the right job to come along.

What Goes Wrong with the First Job

Business lore is filled with examples of the tenuous nature of an individual's first job. Studies have been made that indicate the vast majority of people do not hold their first job for long. The failure rate is high.

Indeed, many employers refuse to hire anyone who has not previously been employed elsewhere. Such employers see no reason why they should pay the price for furnishing the employees all of their training and also pay the price for the trainees' errors. As one top-flight executive said, "I like to catch them on their third or fourth bounce after they've had all the delusions kicked out of them about what business is really about. There is no way in the world I am going to hire a man early in his career. I agree with George Allen (the former Washington Redskins football coach) when he says he only wants veterans, he's not interested in paying the price of bringing up rookies." Unquestionably, rookies are a big risk, so what goes wrong in the relationship between the rookie and the employer? Well, several things. Mistakes are made by both parties. Neither the employee nor the employer is wholly innocent in this matter. What goes wrong?

THE JOB HAS BEEN OVERSOLD

Frequently, in its eagerness to hire bright, young, promising people, the company grossly oversells not only it-

---

Your Career

self but the position it has to offer. Not uncommonly, executives paint glowing pictures of company growth and glory, promising the recruit rapid advancement in a challenging field. So it is not too surprising that the individual becomes disenchanted with his or her inglorious situation after a few months of stacking boxes in a supermarket. Perhaps nowhere was this practice so widely misused as in recruiting recent college graduates. The firms were grossly overselling themselves, promising what they could not deliver. Thus, it was only natural that the individual became disillusioned rather rapidly.

The wise employer deliberately undersells the job. One entrepreneur goes out of the way to paint a bleak picture for the recruit with the thought that the individual will be far happier when he learns that the truth is considerably brighter than he expected.

It is natural for the employer to want to paint a rosy picture of the company's situation. And remember that often the person trying to hire you is being paid to hire people. Top management hired the personnel manager to staff the organization—hire the people. If he fails to hire enough people, he may lose his job.

THE TRUTH IS HIDDEN

Closely akin to overselling is deliberately hiding the truth from the recruit. Some companies promise the individual a salary that simply cannot be achieved. Others make promises they cannot fulfill. One bright young lady was grossly unhappy with her department store employer, for she had been assured a position in fashion merchandising but found herself mired down as a buyer in housewares. The employer kept explaining that he had all sorts of buyers for fashions but he did not have any good housewares buyers. He was only interested in her as a housewares buyer; however, he did not want to tell her the truth when hiring her for fear of losing her. There is the rather quaint notion among some deceitful executives that if they can lure the person to work for them under some pretense, then once the person is on the job, he can be sold any bill of goods. So these employers are willing to say whatever it takes to get the person aboard, relying upon their powers of persuasion and personality to sell the individual into available slots. This does not lead to a good working relationship.

THE REALITY IS NOT AS EXPECTED

One of the more common causes of initial disillusionment is the individual's ultimate revelation that the reality he thought he wanted was not actually what he really desired. For years Harry wanted to be a CPA; all his education was aimed toward the goal of becoming a certified public accountant. He finally achieved that esteemed objective and went to work for a large CPA concern, one of the big eight. His first job was to audit a fish hatchery. Yes, you guessed it: he spent one month counting fish in all the pools. That was all he did—count fish! His next job was scant better: he was in charge of auditing the expense accounts for 5,000 sales representatives. And so it went for several assignments. Each time he was given a task entailing some dull audit job of counting or checking up on something. Finally, the reality hit him. He did not like the work. It was not what he really wanted to do. The reality of being a CPA was totally different than his preconceived notions of the job. Now don't jump to the conclusion that he based his decision on inadequate input, for he had talked with many of the CPAs who had been with the firm for years and people who were doing truly top-notch managerial CPA work. Still the work was not what he wanted, which gives rise to a question of where he got his ideas of what a certified public accountant did for a living. However, this is just exactly the problem: a great many people in this world literally have no idea of what it is really like to be a member of a certain profession. Only the reality of the situation drives it home. When they finally stumble upon what it is all about, many of them quit to find other work.

Paula graduated from a large engineering school with a specialty in mechanical engineering. Her first employer, a large aircraft company, put her on a drafting board. Paula quit after a few months, for she was not overly fond of drafting. Paula's next employer, another aerospace concern, found the same niche for her. The root of this problem is, of course, that Paula simply did not take time to investigate and think through carefully the nature of the career she had selected.

This problem seems particularly critical among the millions of young women now aspiring to meaningful business careers. They often make enthusiastic comments one would expect to hear in Hollywood from hopeful starlets. I try to explain that what they are planning to do is go to work, hard work. A business career is not a lark and is not often very exciting or romantic.

THE SPOILED-BRAT SYNDROME

Many failures on the first job are due to the spoiled-brat syndrome in which the individual walks around in a state of shock at having to get up at six o'clock in the morning to get to work by eight and having to put in eight hours doing something. That has not happened before. In school perhaps this person had to make an eight o'clock class a few times, but not likely; more likely he arranged his schedule so that he had nothing before eleven o'clock. He worked about 15 hours a week and spent the rest of the time amusing himself. A great many young people simply have no idea of what it is like to put in a full day's work. They have never had to do it; it comes as a rude shock to them when their first employer feels it is only right that they do so in exchange for their pay.

This is one of the reasons potential employers love to hire individuals with good, tough work experience in their backgrounds. One such employer said, "I like to see a man who has had to work on the railroad or dig ditches or work in a steel mill, for I know he had to put in a hard day's work for his money and that every time he becomes dissatisfied or unhappy with me he is going to think back to those days on the railroad or in the steel mills and give a second thought to telling me where I can go jump." Thus, many people fail on their first jobs simply because they are not prepared to work, they do not know what work is, and they are not ready to accept it.

Second, the spoiled brat has been nursed along all his life, throughout his entire educational experience. For sixteen years he has worked under the doting supervision of teachers who told him what to do and when to do it. Suddenly he is thrust into the business world and into a situation where perhaps he is expected to do some things without being told. In many cases, he is on his own and expected to show results. He does not know what to do because there is no teacher to tell him, so he quits his job to look for someone to nurse him along.

Third, there is the dirty-work aspect. A great number of jobs have a certain amount of dirty work connected with them. There is no escaping it—someone must carry out the garbage of the world. Someone must do all the unpleasant things that need to be done. In a retail store someone cleans the house and straightens stock and marks goods in and takes care of things that nobody is particularly fond of doing. Now guess who is going to do this. Do you think for one moment that a boss is going to be particularly keen to do it when he or she is paying you good money for standing around? Don't be ridiculous! You will be expected to do the dirty work. The boss had to do it coming up and sees no reason why he ought to do it now.

One of the basic principles of most organizations is that the low man on the totem pole can expect to get saddled with the unpleasant tasks. However, many tender young things are repelled at being asked to do such menial jobs and quit to look for executive positions. Indeed, if you really want to impress an employer, be eager to do the dirty work that must be done. Dig in and show the boss that you are not afraid to get your hands dirty. One top executive with a very large company recently said to me as we were down in a warehouse lifting some boxes, handling a certain emergency one Sunday, "Anytime I get so big for my britches that I refuse to get down and work when work must be done, then it's time for me to quit."

BAD JOBS

Before you jump to the conclusion that the general tenor of this section is that the failure in a first job is largely due to the individual's inadequacies, let me hasten to assure you that probably is not so.

There are bad jobs, contrary to what some mythologists would have you believe. There are jobs that are simply no good, have no future, are woefully underpaid, and the individual simply is not gaining anything useful from them. About all you can say about the position is that it pays a certain amount of money and that is all.

There are bad companies—firms going no place but down; the people with them are going to suffer. There are companies whose policies are such that there is little reason for an employee to stay with them. An example: one top-flight stockbroker was enticed to take the presidency of an investment underwriting concern. He quit at the end of two weeks with the statement, "This outfit is crooked! I want no part of it." He was right, as the principal owners of the concern were eventually indicted by the SEC and imprisoned. He had correctly spotted very early in the game that he was working with a very bad company and he bailed out as quickly as possible, thus saving himself a great deal of grief.

Bad situations exist in good companies. Polly was working for one of the better companies in the nation as a sales representative. She had been quite successful in one territory and had been promoted to assistant branch manager in another. However, this new position brought her under a branch manager who was terrible. Polly and the branch manager did not get along well at all, and top management would do nothing about the situation for various reasons of policy. Polly was stuck in a really terrible situation—one that was wrecking home and happiness—thus it was not surprising that she resigned to accept employment elsewhere. Individuals can find themselves in predicaments peculiar to their particular situation and be forced to leave, even though the company and the job may be excellent.

Common Mistakes Made in First Jobs

I see four major mistakes people make in their first few jobs. Some people never stop making these mistakes.

YOU ARE NOT THE PRESIDENT

Sometimes it seems exceedingly difficult to get the idea across to the new employee that he is not the boss. He is not running the show; it is not his company, it is someone else's. Yet the individual has the idea that he is running the place, he has his ideas of how operations ought to be, and his own ideas of various procedures. He is unwilling to accept being the employee and the other fellow as the boss. Typically, tenure in such situations is short-lived.

THERE IS A REASON WHY THEY DO IT THAT WAY

If I but had a dime for every time I have heard some young person complaining about company practices, I would be an extremely wealthy man today. In the typical case the individual comes in off the street, new to the job, and immediately sees all sorts of things that are not being done as he feels they should be done. Procedures look stupid and inefficient to him; there certainly must be a better way to do these things. He knows a better way—knows exactly how they should be done. Well, perhaps he is right; maybe there is a better way to do whatever it is he wants done.

However, there are usually good reasons why the firm is doing things its own way. Probably the executives have given a great deal of thought to the problem and the way things are being done is a compromise. It comes back to the systems approach. The young person is looking at one part of a system and thinks he ought to change that system for his convenience, not realizing that in making one change everything else in the system must change also and that the trade-offs are unbalanced and unfavorable for the firm. Thus, it is strongly advisable that the individual refrain from giving his patent medicine solutions to the problems he sees until he really comprehends the whole system and that, in fact, he does have a viable and practical solution to the problem. Notice that I am not saying the individual should not make constructive suggestions for improvement of operations. Certainly such suggestions, if they are soundly conceived and practical, mark an individual for advancement, for that is exactly what management expects. However, few things can harm one's career more quickly than to gain the reputation of shooting wildly from the hip, offering half-baked solutions to complex problems.

UNREALISTIC EXPECTATIONS

Many problems the individual perceives on a first job are simply the result of unrealistic expectations. He expects big raises too soon and expects a promotion far sooner than reality permits. He expects his work to be interesting and challenging, when in fact it is routine. In short, the person's expectations are simply unrealistic, thus disappointment is inevitable.

IMPATIENCE

One prominent lawyer maintained, "I think possibly the most valuable asset for a successful career in business is patience. I see businessmen who have gotten into messes simply because they were too impatient. They just had to rush things or push things through and in doing so, made all sorts of mistakes. I also see a great many people making very unwise settlements in negotiations, simply because they haven't the patience it takes to conduct sound negotiations."

There is much truth to this lawyer's statement since patience has its place. Many people simply do not realize that it takes a certain amount of time to learn a job and that one is not given pay increases and promotions when he expects them. Actually, a case can be made that one is always underpaid in business, for you are not likely to get your pay increases until after you have earned them. Many times the individual is simply not willing to wait out the red tape and put in the time necessary for achieving success in one's line of endeavor. It is very difficult for the young person to be told that he or she is too young for a job when in fact, in many instances that is the case. The employer is simply not going to turn over a responsible position to someone of a tender age just on basic policy. After all, the boss is trying to cover himself too, for he would be sharply criticized by superiors if he were to place a new employee in charge of a critical operation and have it fail.

The Basic Formula: H.E.W.

Success on the first job is really the result of a simple formula—H.E.W. H = Honest, E = Effective Operations, and W = Work. Thus, while it sounds like an old-fashioned, puritan sermon, the fact still remains that success in your first job depends upon working hard, being as effective as possible, and developing a reputation for being honest.

HONESTY

You will not go very far if you are not basically honest, for the dishonest individual is discovered sooner or later by his coworkers and must leave, because no one really cares to do business with a crook. If a potential employer has any reason to doubt your basic honesty, you'll not likely get much of a hearing. Even some harmless lies on the application blank will give the employer reason to wonder where the applicant's deceptions will stop.

EFFECTIVE OPERATIONS

Some people work long hours and work very hard, but they do not seem to be effective at producing; some blockage exists between the effort they put forth and the results they get. They have not learned how to be effective. The more effective people are, the less time they have to spend working, for they can attain high output without putting in long hours. Effectiveness is a complex matter which we will get to in a later section, but you must learn to be effective and that means getting results, which, incidentally, often means getting along with people. To be effective, you frequently must be able to get other people to do what you ask of them.

WORK

Some people consider work the dirtiest, most obscene, vulgar four-letter word in our language. In all our sophisticated talk about success on the job, we tend to overlook the role of work. Most of the time the person with the most successful career has simply worked hardest at it. Those of you who are cynical about the relationship of hard work and success simply do not see how much some people work, for it is hidden from your vision. You do not see them working at night, on weekends, or early in the morning, for you are not around when they are working.

Make no mistake about it, employers are greatly impressed by young people who are willing to work hard. That means getting down to work early in the morning and leaving late at night, being willing to work at nights and on weekends.

It is not very likely that a person will go very far unless he or she is willing to put forth work. Some people have mediocre minds and talent, yet they go far in the business world simply because they are willing to work hard at it. Indeed, this is the only explanation for the success of many people, for when you casually meet them they have little going for them mentally, but they have been willing to pay the price and work hard in their professions.

About Pay and Promotions

As you expected, pay and promotions are important, but they may be even more important to your career than you had realized, for they are something other than money. The average employee wants a promotion because it means more pay and more goodies, and there the average bloke stops thinking. Pay and promotions are a lot more than money. They are communications. When you are promoted, your boss is communicating something to you that is concrete and definite, and you have tangible evidence of your achievements. When your boss raises your pay more than can be expected because of normal seniority, he is putting his thoughts about you in tangible form.

One young man learned his lesson the hard way. For four years he worked for a boss who regularly patted him on the head and told him what a good boy he was, how happy he was with his work, that he was doing an excellent job, that he would soon be promoted, and that riches would start coming his way. A year passed and nothing happened. Two years passed and still nothing happened. Three years passed and he was still being told what a good worker he was, but he had nothing in his paycheck or title to show for it. Finally, after four years, the man wised-up and left for more promising pastures. Words are cheap; it costs the boss nothing to tell you how great you are and make promises to keep you quiet and busy working at whatever it is he wants you to do. But if the words are not backed up with actions, you are being told nothing. Believe the actions, don't believe the words. Tacitly, the top-notch employee is thinking, when told how great he is, "Don't tell me, put it in my paycheck."

PAY AND PROMOTIONS AS STATUS SYMBOLS

In a very real sense, your status within the organization and your relationships with other people depend in large part upon your rank and pay. People judge your importance and your status by your title and by how much the company is paying you. These are the only tangible handles people have to evaluate just how important you are. Thus they serve as a communications device to tell the world who and what you are.

Many times I have heard tales from middle management executives relating that they are doing the work of some senior position but have not been given the title nor the money for doing it. A rather odd thing about these people: I have yet to run into one who is happy with the situation or who really lasted long with the organization in such an arrangement. One middle management executive was being made the vice-president of a large company. He was discussing the matter with a very close friend who was president of a large competing firm. The friend told the man, "Make sure they give you the money that goes with the position. They are both important. If you don't get the money, your status among the vice-presidential group will be unworkable."

Bear in mind that every pay raise and every promotion goes on your record and becomes a most important part of your resume. Future employers are going to make an evaluation about your talents from it. One of the most important records that you can show is rapid rise in both rank and pay within a company, for advancement is evidence that your superiors thought a great deal of your talents. Conversely, if you work for someone for a few years and have little to show for it, that void is certainly a black mark against you, for it meant those people did not think much of your work.

WHAT IS A PROMOTION?

It would be amusing, if it were not so pathetic, to hear people tell of being promoted when, in fact nothing happened to them—their bosses simply changed their titles. One publishing employee was beaming over her promotion to field editor. I questioned her at some length about the change in the nature of her work or if she had been given a raise. Neither had happened. The woman was so hungry for status that she readily accepted her change in title as being a promotion. It was not, but evidently it fed her ego for a while.

Many people think they are being promoted when in fact, they are only being moved sideways. Some are even being demoted, yet management has been so clever that the individual interprets the move as a promotion. One rather abrasive young man, who headed up a division, had built its volume from two million to eight million dollars in a period of three years. He was justifiably proud of this accomplishment. However, management was out of tune with this individual, for they regarded him as a bit too brash and outspoken for their likes. He was offered a "promotion" to manage another division that was in trouble but he accepted the new challenge all too readily. He came to realize that he had not been promoted at all; the new job had less status, was a smaller operation than the one he had been heading, and in the end he had to leave the company, for in reality he had been demoted. One salesman for a large office supplies manufacturer was being "promoted" to manager of the North Dakota territory. Again, the move was a demotion. They moved the man into the Badlands and out of a large potential market. They threw him a title just to make the move less painful.

So be advised that all changes carrying higher sounding titles are not necessarily promotions. The old story about getting rid of problems by promoting them upward has a great deal of validity to it. Many corporate presidents have been promoted to chairman of the board, or chairman of the executive committee only to find themselves without any power. You had better learn how to recognize a valid promotion. A true promotion carries more responsibility for doing more important work for a higher salary than the job you now hold.

PROMOTIONS ARE A BIG PROBLEM

Here you must be able to see things from the viewpoint of your boss, for promotions are a big problem to employers. Often several people are eligible for a promotion, but only one can have it, and the others will be disappointed. In other instances some very worthy people may deserve promotions, but circumstances simply provide no openings—a most frustrating situation for the diligent administrator. In a very real way, seldom is a promotion available when the individual deserves it. There is always a time lag. You can expect to spend some time in a situation in which you deserve a promotion but none is forthcoming. This is particularly true in smaller concerns. Large growth concerns normally have enough slots open above to allow room for the individual when it comes time to be promoted, but not always.

Moreover, the classic seniority problem is culturally built into our society. For this reason, people on the job the longest feel they have the most right to be considered for promotion solely on that basis. Anytime the boss promotes someone over another person eligible for the job on the basis of seniority, a certain amount of trouble can be expected. Thus bosses are strongly tempted, all other things being equal, to promote on the basis of seniority, and even in cases where everything else is not equal. Many times the younger person must clearly be superior to get promoted over an older person. Clearly, then, the promotion process is loaded with difficulties for the administrator. Ill-advised promotions can cause a great deal of grief. Moreover, administrators can lose many good employees by failure to adequately recognize them at the time for promotions and pay raises.

THE ART OF GETTING PROMOTED

Many people do not get promoted simply because they do not know how to go about it. Let us talk about some of the tactics that can facilitate your rise.

Often the only way the individual can gain a promotion or pay increase is to have a bona fide outside offer from another firm and tacitly use it as an ultimatum: "Promote me or I'll go elsewhere." And many times the individual can only get recognition by going elsewhere, for it is not to be had in the present position. Thus, when using an outside offer in a hold-up play, you must be very certain that you are willing to accept the other job. You must be prepared to go elsewhere. This is not the place to bluff.

One tragic example comes to mind. Many years ago an old Big-10 football coach was most happily settled in his university. He had been there for many years and his colleagues loved him dearly, although he did not really turn out many winning teams. Nevertheless, his reputation earned him a standing offer from one professional team to become its head coach, which he had turned down several years in a row. Then one year he won the Big-10 title. He met with the board of trustees and made them aware of the pro club offer and they raised his salary handsomely. The next year he had a so-so season; nevertheless, he returned to the board of trustees with an even better offer from the professional club. This time they handed him his hat and said so long, it's been good to know you. He had to accept the professional coaching job. His family would not move from the college town with him so he went alone. He died shortly thereafter, a very unhappy individual, for he really did not want to leave that university. He dearly loved his job with them, but he had just never learned when to bluff and when not to bluff. You must never bluff when you are not prepared to accept having the bluff called, for that is always a distinct possibility.

A word is due about using outside offers to gain your way. If you try a direct hold-up play by walking into the boss's office, laying the offer on his desk and, in essence, telling him to "pay up or I'll leave," chances are you will be handed your hat. Not many people like to be blackmailed in such a manner, for once it becomes known around the organization that the way to a promotion or pay increase is to threaten the boss with an outside offer, then the boss can expect a long line at his door with outside offers for his attention. From a policy standpoint, he simply cannot run his business this way. He must set his wage and salary policies and more or less stick by them. No, the adroit person finds other ways of communicating the outside offer to the boss. Let other people in the organization who want you to stay convey the message to the boss. "We better get on the ball or we're going to lose good old George."

Another tactic for getting promoted is to somehow get the person to vacate the position to which you aspire. Perhaps you may help to get him or her promoted, thus giving you an opportunity for the job. Or, the person may find a better job or even get fired.

About Your Boss

If it has not yet occurred to you that your boss plays an important role in your career, then you are indeed in grave difficulty. The goodies flow downward. They are bestowed upon you by your superiors—your bosses. A good boss, one who appreciates your talents, can do many good things for your career. A poor one can do it much harm. Admit it: bosses are important! Unfortunately, not many of us really understand bosses very well, so a few words might be in order concerning the care and feeding of bosses.

THE BOSS IS A HUMAN BEING, TOO

Contrary to the opinions voiced by many people, the boss is also a human being. He or she has personal feelings, perhaps a family, personal problems of all sorts, and bleeds the same as everyone else. This mundane observation is made because I never cease to be amazed by the number of people who will confront the boss acting as if he had no feelings whatsoever. They do not seem to comprehend that the boss will react to events and confrontations emotionally, much as anyone else will. The problem arises from the ability of many bosses to hide their feelings. In advancing through the ranks they learned to project an unemotional, unflappable facade. They learned to keep a straight face, a level head, and a quiet voice in the face of extremely provoking circumstances. Indeed, many times the more provoked they become, the more placid their overt behavior appears to be. One outstanding executive, when truly provoked, would smile and laugh as a countermeasure. Although somewhat amusing, it was a most disarming tactic. Inside he could be absolutely boiling mad at the other person, but only the smile on his face was apparent. Thus be warned that although many bosses have learned to hide their true feelings, they still have them. Perhaps even more so, for they usually have rather well-developed egos if they are any good at all. If you think for one minute that you can hand the boss a lot of garbage and get away with it, you'd better think again. At least one career was ruined by such nonsense.

A particularly bright subordinate was not overly fond of his boss, a well-respected man with a good, nationwide reputation. One night the subordinate, perhaps urged on by too much alcohol, told the boss what he thought of him, which was not much. The boss merely smiled, not saying a word. The subordinate's stay with the firm was short. Moreover, he gave the young man extremely bad recommendations throughout that rather small industry. The man had to change his career goals. One just does not go around kicking Santa Claus in the shins if one wants a merry Christmas.

THE BOSS HAS A CAREER, TOO

The boss has his own career and career problems, also. Everyone has a boss—your boss has a boss and that boss has a boss. Everyone reports to someone and is concerned about the relationship. If you pose a threat to your boss's career, he will likely try to do something about it. If you are helping him to advance his career, he will love you for it, for cooperation sets up the basis for the contract between you and your boss.

HE NEEDS YOU—YOU NEED HIM

A good, sound basis for any contract is that the buyer and seller need each other; both benefit from the contract. So it is with a job. You benefit from the company and the company benefits from you. Substitute "boss" for "company" and the same holds true: you need the boss and the boss needs you. If he does not need you, then you had better start looking for employment elsewhere, for someday it will dawn on him and he will rectify the situation. The more he needs you, the more obviously secure you are. However, there are dangers lurking when you become so vital to your boss that he cannot do without you. If he is totally dependent on you, he may block your promotion or advancement, for he needs you right where you are. The dangers of this situation are very similar to the days in the Navy when the wise ones avoided becoming essential—a sailor who became essential was frozen in his job and was not discharged when his points came up.

SPONSORSHIP

A sponsor is someone who takes a liking to you and decides to help in advancing your career. A young man fresh out of USC Business School decided that he wanted to be a salesman for a men's apparel manufacturer and eventually became a manufacturer's representative handling several lines. He had a little experience selling in a menswear store while he was in college. However, upon graduation he found it difficult to get a job because business conditions were gloomy. Most apparel manufacturers were looking for someone with five to ten years' experience; they wanted to hire someone who knew the territory.

The young man walked into the Dallas Apparel Mart one day shortly before market week and, after searching around, entered the sales office of one sales representative and volunteered his services, "I'll work for you for free just for the experience." The rep was overwhelmed. He had never had anyone offer to work for nothing but the experience. He took the lad on to help during market week but insisted on paying him. Things went extremely well. The young man was a big help and actually handled several large accounts successfully. The rep claimed, "He worked many accounts better than I could have worked them." The rep was so impressed that he sponsored the young man. He told everyone around the Mart how well the young man performed. Moreover, he lined up interviews for him with six leading firms. The young man had picked up a sponsor and he soon had a job.

Sponsors are invaluable, for they can say things about you that you cannot say for yourself. Moreover, they are believed, for a sponsor has no apparent reason for lying. No financial interest is involved. A good sponsor can do a great deal for your career. But what is a good sponsor? A good sponsor is someone well connected in the industry with opinions that are respected. It does little good to be sponsored by some ne'er-do-well whose opinions and words mean little to those in the industry. Being sponsored by such people can actually hurt because one becomes associated with them in the minds of others. In the academic world one is well advised to study under someone with a known reputation for turning out top-flight individuals.

One might wonder why people volunteer to become sponsors. Well, this works two ways. The sponsor of a bright young person who turns out well has made two friends. He has made a good friend of the person sponsored, which can come back to benefit him many times over. Moreover, if the person proves worthy—is everything he or she claimed to be—then the employer is grateful, thus the sponsor is twice blessed. Many people simply like to help others with deserving talent advance.

Uninformed people are sometimes shocked to learn how saturated our system is with the practice of sponsorship. Most of the top-flight people in this country are in the top positions because they were sponsored by someone. Someone blessed them and helped them rise. There is an old saying, "You can't do it by yourself, you need help." That is true, and a good sponsor can give you the help you need.

Bear in mind that you are not a passive pawn in this matter. Some persons seek out good sponsors. They go to certain schools, take certain courses, and make great efforts to become friends with those from whom they want help. Many times they are rather aggressive about it, but if they are talented, it may not matter. Bear in mind that the sponsor relationship places an obligation upon you. You owe your sponsor allegiance and support. One industry leader sponsored a bright young man who quickly rose in the industry. Thereafter he hardly recognized his sponsor and their relationship was severed. The ingrate suffered in many ways from the loss, although he never realized it.

Bear in mind also that many benefits apt to come your way never do so because they were blocked by someone. Most of the time you will never be aware of what you do not get. In the case above, the young man was proposed as an officer of an industry trade association but the ex-sponsor made a few remarks to kill that thought. Just be advised that you owe a debt to your sponsor and few things sour the relationship so readily as overt signs of ingratitude.

WHAT IS A GOOD BOSS?

Since bosses come in all sizes and shapes—some good, some bad, most mediocre, perhaps a few words are needed to describe a good boss so at least you will recognize one when you have one. It is discouraging to see someone working for an excellent boss without knowing it. A good boss:

> does not stand in your way
> gives promotions when deserved
> gives you deserved recognition
> protects you
> trains you
> is fair

knows you

works at the job

provides leadership

is politically adept in organizations

will not stand in your way

A very personable man not too long out of a Big-10 football factory became head coach at a leading university after spending the needed years as an assistant coach. He was quickly successful largely because of four very talented assistants he was able to hire. It would be impossible to convey here just how good these assistants were, but they quickly provided the school with a championship football team. However, this young coach had several character flaws, one of which was that he blocked the advancement of his assistants. As the abilities of his assistant coaches became known, several schools were interested in hiring them as head coaches. As is customary in the college football industry, the athletic director of the hiring school will first contact the athletic director and the head coach before contacting the assistant coach. This procedure is a matter of ethics and more practically, a matter of getting information. The interested school would ask the head coach, "Is so-and-so ready to be a head coach yet?" The young boss would uniformly reply, "No, he is a good line coach but he hasn't got the whole picture yet," which was correct in one case but wrong in regard to the other three assistants. Eventually this "back-stabbing" got back to the assistant coaches, as it usually does. That was the straw that broke the camel's back. The assistant coaches started talking, for they had lost their love for their leader; and the NCAA listened. The head coach is no longer a coach.

A good boss does not stand in the way of his subordinates. He goes out of his way to promote them, for a good boss knows he can get other good subordinates. Look at the record of Bud Wilkinson, former head coach at the University of Oklahoma, for developing head coaches. Anytime a school would contact Coach Wilkinson about one of his assistants he would give them a truthful, excellent recommendation. His subordinates loved him.

Promotions Recognition is one factor most employees consider important. Few things destroy relationships more quickly than the inability or refusal of a boss to recognize good performance either through promotion, if possible, or pay increases. Even a pat on the back is welcome. Organizational morale is badly damaged by unwise promotions. If the boss promoted someone known to be unqualified into a job over some qualified and deserving person, not much good will come of the change. Promotions are touchy affairs. Ego involvement is tremendous. When people are turned down for promotions, their egos are badly damaged; they have been rejected. They are likely to look elsewhere for work. Perhaps their bosses are trying to tell them that. Still, a good boss carefully manages the reward system and tries to reward appropriately those who deserve to be rewarded.

Protect You Yes, employees want protection—from other people in the organization and from the boss's boss. One head of a purchasing department did not last very long when she failed to realize this aspect of the job. The various purchasing agents were being harassed daily by everyone in the organization. People in every department were screaming at them for this or that. Moreover, they were being discriminated against in parking and other perquisites of corporate life. The head of the department was so concerned with her own career and her own security that she did not go to bat for her employees.

A good boss would tell the people in other departments, "If you have a bitch about any of my people tell me and I'll handle it, but you leave my people alone!" Moreover, good bosses support their people to make certain that they get their share of rewards. The people in the trenches need someone to fight their battles for them in higher echelons.

Trains you The importance of training has already been established. A good boss conscientiously tries to develop your talents and to bring out the best in you. He is concerned about training you. A poor boss does not give a damn whether or not you develop. All he wants is for you to keep your nose clean and do your job.

Fairness Practically all surveys on what constitutes a good boss disclose the matter of fairness, whatever that may be. The concept of fairness is most elusive. It is difficult to determine what is fair. Nevertheless, deep down everyone has a code; a boss can do certain things that the employee will consider to be unfair.

Roy worked long and hard building up his sales territory by working weekends and nights pounding the pavement. After three years he had quadrupled the volume from that territory. The sales manager looked at the record and decided that Roy had more territory than he really needed and divided it into four territories. Roy was right back where he had started. Since he was on commission, his pay suffered commensurately. He learned the lesson that many sales reps have learned operating under such managerial tactics: it is pointless to work hard building up your territory for if you do, it will simply be taken away from you. You will not be allowed to keep the benefits you worked so hard to earn. Most sales people consider this to be most unfair and their performance suffers as a result.

Knows You Few bosses really know their subordinates. They are so mired down with their own problems that they do not take the time to get to know their employees, yet good management requires such knowledge. It is difficult to know how to manage people intelligently unless you do know something about them. Good bosses will take time to get to know their people.

Works at the Job Until you have worked for a boss who is seldom around and who doesn't get his work done, you'll not likely fully appreciate the importance of this attribute. It can be most frustrating and aggravating for your efforts to be held up simply because your boss doesn't do his or her job. Unfortunately, this happens all too frequently. Some people naively think that once they become boss they no longer have to work very hard. Experience will show that the opposite is true. Bosses often have to work harder and longer than their subordinates.

Provides Leadership Leadership entails a wide range of things worthy of a sizeable book. It is sufficient to say here that leadership skills are rare. Few bosses are real leaders, most are plodders and followers. But if you're lucky enough to have a great leader for a boss you just may be led into greatness. Unquestionably a good boss will lead you to achieve greater results than you would be able to obtain on your own.

Politically Adept in Organizations If you and your group are to prosper, you'll need resources and a boss who is politically well wired in the organization. If your boss does not enjoy a good political position in the organization, you'll pay part of the price for his ineptness. And you'll benefit in many ways if your boss has some clout.

Your pay and promotions will be larger and quicker if your boss's recommendations go unchallenged.

GETTING THE BOSS FIRED

Yes, you can get the boss fired; it happens all the time. Many bosses hold very tenuous positions. Sometimes a group of dissatisfied employees will go around their boss with a bill of particulars indicting him. Accusations sometimes work, more times they do not. One group of dissatisfied employees, eight of them to be exact, were unhappy with their chief engineer. They presented the president with a list of grievances one April 1st (a venture thereafter referred to in the organization as the "March of the April Fools"). The general message conveyed to the president was that they did not think much of the chief engineer's abilities. They thought they had extracted a promise from the president not to tell the chief engineer about their visit. However, the minute they had left, the president called the chief engineer to tell him all about it and ratify his support for him. These employees had the amazing inability to understand why thereafter that chief engineer did them dirty at every opportunity.

If you are going to go up against the boss, make sure you have the guns to win the battle. If you lose it, you had best be prepared to move elsewhere, since life certainly will not be very comfortable where you are. Never wound a king! However, you must understand that in most instances you cannot win such battles. Conspiracy is a bad tactic, for conspirators are normally discovered.

Most top executives simply will not listen to your story. Oh, they will politely sit there, nod, and make a few noises, but from a management standpoint, top executives cannot run an organization well if they undercut the authority of their immediate subordinates by welcoming complaints from their subordinates' subordinates. If employees in an organization learn that they can get a superior into difficulty or even fired by getting the ear of the top executive, then the top executive will be listening to many such delegations. He will quickly find it difficult to hire good middle management. Who wants to work for a boss who encourages the rank and file to jump around him willy-nilly? This is why the armed forces and most organizations insist on the observance of a definite chain of command. Granted, although there are situations where one feels compelled to jump around that chain, still there are better ways to do it than the formal confrontation. Thus, the chances are that the conspirators will lose in any such tactic. But even if they win they lose, for no one likes a conspirator. The next superior no doubt will be aware of these conspirators and may remove them as threats. Moreover, once they have conspired to destroy one superior they will find it difficult to do so again, for they would seem ridiculous crybabies if they presented the top executive with another list of grievances concerning the replacement for the person they stabbed in the first place. No, overt conspiracies are stupid.

Now let us see how Howard got his bosses fired—three of them—all in the name of advancing his own career. This young engineer, fresh out of MIT, went to work for an aerospace concern as a rather lowly draftsman and general flunky. He was talented and quietly ambitious. His superior came to rely upon him for many things. More and more Howard was doing his boss's work while the boss played. Howard encouraged this by continually assuring his boss that he would cover for him and, for a short while, he did so magnificently. Soon the boss was absenting himself every nice afternoon to research the flight characteristics of a small, white, dimpled sphere after being struck by a long stick. These absences did not go unnoticed, for in the normal course of business, people try to reach you and when they repeatedly cannot, they begin to ask questions. Finally the big boss asked Howard where the department head was. Howard told him the straightforward truth, exactly what was going on. The department head was fired and Howard got his boss's job.

Howard, now a department head, obtained a better position with another aerospace concern and the second verse was similar to the first. His new superior came to rely upon Howard's talents and Howard encouraged his extracurricular activities, which this time turned toward the horses rather than golf. Soon Howard had the superior's job when management saw what was happening. Howard had many little ways to make certain that the top management became aware of his superiors' absences, ways in which Howard was not connected. Then Howard became head of quality control for another aerospace concern. His boss was vice-president over the entire branch plant. This story has a different twist to it, for Howard managed to get his boss's job by stabbing him in the back, quietly and subtly. The vice-president signed a large contract that contained a sizeable error, one not in the company's favor. Howard knew of the error but since he was not connected with it in any way, he let his superior sign the mistake. Of course, he played innocent all the way. When the corporate top management became aware of this negligence, Howard was the new vice-president.

This entire story was spoken by Howard. He bragged about climbing into top management over the bodies of his three superiors. For those goody-goody moralists

---

who might be appalled at Howard's climb, let us hasten to point out that our system may be better off for such behavior. Why do we want incompetent people holding down managerial positions, who want to play golf while letting subordinates do their work, or who are careless in their jobs? Howard was making the competitive system work by eliminating those who would not do their jobs properly. It might be added that Howard was most competent technically and was well regarded by his subordinates, none of whom was able to "stab him in the back."

WHAT THE BOSS WANTS FROM YOU

We talked previously about what you want from your boss, but it is more important for you to realize what your boss wants from you. Your boss also expects a few things.

Do Your Job First and foremost, your boss expects you to do your job the right way. You are expected to work. There is no substitute for work. There are jobs to do and work to be done; bosses have a way of becoming nasty when subordinates fail to complete the work. Bear in mind that a good boss has long since learned failure has many excuses. Talk to anyone who has failed to do the job and you will hear all sorts of plausible reasons why it was not done, but they are all beside the point. The only important thing is that the job was not done; the reasons are not important. The most valuable image you can develop is that of getting the job done, no matter what. No excuses, no alibis. You must complete the job.

Loyalty Bosses expect loyalty. Unfortunately, many times they expect more loyalty than is due. Nevertheless, their egos expect their people to love them and to be loyal. Few things will upset an administrator more quickly than learning that a subordinate has been disloyal, even through such disloyalty may be helpful to the organization. A sheriff in one Texas county was extremely bitter at his deputies for testifying before the grand jury about his various misdeeds in public office. The fact that the sheriff was a crook seemed not to enter into the discussion at all. He felt they owed him loyalty, no matter what he did. Still, despite all of the factual, realistic forces preventing subordinates from really being loyal to anyone but themselves, superiors strongly prize the appearance of loyalty in their subordinates. It is critical that you appear to be loyal. Whether in fact you truly are is your own business.

Disloyalty can take many forms. Perhaps an individual carries tales outside the department, telling stories the boss does not want told. Perhaps he fails to support a boss's ideas properly. Perhaps he asks for a transfer to another department. Perhaps he bad-mouthed the boss socially. Whatever, such things eventually find their way back to the boss. Once the boss becomes convinced of someone's disloyalty, he will probably try to remove that individual from the organization. Most administrators feel that it is very important to have people working for them who are reasonably loyal and in whom they can reasonably confide with some degree of assurance that they are not going to be stabbed in the back.

Honesty Any evidence that the employee is dishonest is usually dealt with quickly and harshly. No one wants a crook on the payroll.

Integrity Integrity includes, but goes beyond, honesty. It concerns truthfulness, ethical behavior, morality, being true to one's own philosophies, refusal to sacrifice morality for the sake of expediency, and keeping one's word. Integrity is prized by most top executives of quality.

Compatibility The boss expects his people to be able to work with one another satisfactorily and to get along with each other. More people are fired because they are unable to get along with others than for any other reason.

About Changing Jobs

Perhaps one of the most critical decisions one makes is to change jobs. To go or not to go is often the question. This is a critical decision because you are apt to make a mistake that can send your career into a tailspin. Judgments made on these matters are apt to be poor because of their high emotional content. Studies of executive judgment indicate that one is apt to make bad judgments when emotions run high in the matter; usually the emotions are running high when one is contemplating a job change. Let's examine two such decisions that had disastrous consequences.

Jerry had an enviable career in the banking industry. Within a decade he had climbed from assistant vice-president in a small town bank to the presidency of a bank that he founded for a wealthy backer. His new bank was tremendously successful. Jerry basked in the glory it reflected upon him. All seemed to be milk and honey in Jerry's career. However, sub rosa, all was not going well between Jerry and the owner of the bank. Jerry disagreed with some things the owner wanted to do that were not quite within the law. Unfortunately, this particular owner was not very receptive to the idea of having his employees pass judgment on his desires. Things became uncomfortable for Jerry, so he decided to accept the presidency of another bank in a small resort town. That job did not last long because Jerry's wife was extremely unhappy in the new environment. There just was not much for her to do in the town, so she urged Jerry to accept a job offer in Southern California, an area where they had grown up and had many friends.

Jerry eventually became vice-president of a small chain of banks in Southern California. His responsibility was to establish and manage a new branch in one of the beach cities. Jerry executed this responsibility magnificently, but difficulties arose again between himself and the owners, for they did not agree with some of Jerry's plans for expansion. Lest one jump to the conclusion that Jerry was difficult to get along with, it might be said that in each case Jerry was correct according to sound business and banking practices. The owners in these situations were independent businessmen using their banks for their own purposes.

At this point, Jerry was approached by a group of venture capitalists who wanted to own a bank. They were bankrolled most impressively, so Jerry accepted the position with the directions that he locate a bank to be purchased or locate an area where one could be started. About three months into the venture, the capitalists changed their minds about wanting to be in the banking business and Jerry was out. His career was at a halt. He was dead in the water. He had interviews with many other banks, but there just was no overwhelming demand for fifty-year-old bank presidents entitled to a salary of $40,000 a year, at least in a banking system that hires young branch managers for $20,000 a year.

After several months of agony, Jerry decided to try the real estate business. He studied and passed the California real estate examination. The following two years were not the best of times for Jerry. It became quite clear that Jerry was not cut out for the real estate business; he was a banker. After much agonizing and no little depression, Jerry sought help from professional career counselors. After many tests, much talking, and $4,500 had been exchanged, they decided Jerry was destined for better things. He should be a "top corporate financial officer." They developed a campaign to get such a position for him, but to no avail. There were no takers, Jerry was not a high-level corporate financial officer. Jerry was a banker and a good one at that. Finally, after much soul-searching, he listened to a friend who urged him to get back into banking—to accept employment with a good growing concern as a vice-president and work his way up the ladder again, which he is now doing.

Jerry's is a classic case of a person whose career went down the tubes with serious repercussions financially and socially because he began changing jobs too quickly. Each job change was essentially a step downward, but he did not realize it at the time because he was not really taking a new job so much as leaving an old one. When one is in the position of fleeing a scene, the chances for improvement are not good.

Jean was a computer expert with IBM making great money. Some promoters put together one of the new, exotic technical groups based around computer technology and managed to persuade Jean to come to work as a vice-president at a fancy salary, with the promise of riches in the future. Jean undertook the venture, quit IBM, and moved to Southern California. It was belly-up in six months. Jean was out of work for a year and is now struggling in some menial capacity to get back into the mainstream. Her decision to quit IBM was a bad one. Anyone aware of the principles of career management would recognize immediately that such a move was fraught with danger; the likelihood of events happening as they did was near certainty. So let's delve into some of the things that need attention when considering a change in jobs.

GRASS LOOKS GREENER

No doubt you have heard this before, but hear it again: the grass usually looks greener on the other side of the fence. You know all of the problems in your own concern, as you live with them daily. Many people can only see the disadvantages of their present situation while overlooking the advantages. You usually only look for the advantages of the new job and seldom see where the bodies are buried. Moreover, psychologically one is apt to ignore all of the trouble signals, the warning flags about the new job. You want to believe that the new job is just what you have been looking for. You want to believe that the grass is greener on the other side of the fence, and you will believe what you want.

While investigating carefully and considering new jobs is of some protection, still it will not keep you from falling prey to this grass-is-greener illusion. Try to keep in mind that what you are looking at is probably not nearly as attractive as you think. Not only will you be unaware of many problems, but things seldom go as planned, so be advised that the new job is almost never as attractive as you think it is. Moreover, your own job is seldom as bad as you think. You probably have a better job than you realize; your emotional reaction to a few irritants blinds you to the total picture. Thus the prospective job should be clearly and substantially better than your present one if you are to have much of a chance of offsetting the green-grass illusion.

DO NOT BELIEVE WHAT YOU HEAR

That people lie should come as no surprise to you. When someone is trying to attract you to a new job, he may tell you whatever it takes to get you. The old saying that misery loves company is so with people in bad situations.

They want to get good people into their bad situations, possibly in the hope of changing things for the better, or simply because it is their job to hire people. Thus, you simply cannot blindly believe anything that the other person tells you. Everything needs to be verified, and you must use some gumption in evaluating it.

PIE IN THE SKY

This section should not be necessary, but evidently it is. It is amazing to see the numbers of people lured from good jobs by impossible, pie-in-the-sky promises. Promoters come along offering the moon to the individual, making promises that cannot possibly be kept, yet people believe them because they want to believe them. Many people want to believe that they can become rich overnight with little work. They want their dreams and will fight desperately if you try to shatter them. Thus, when the pie man comes down the street chanting his song, usually many people will respond to it. You should have learned by now that there are no such things as Santa Claus or the Easter Bunny. No one is interested in making you rich or giving you something for nothing, so if someone starts promising you riches you are most likely being deceived.

THERE COMES A TIME

On a different note, admittedly in many careers there comes a time to change jobs. You have been in one slot for too long and are going to seed. There are jobs in which, for one reason or another, you are going nowhere; perhaps it is your fault, perhaps not. Whichever it is matters not. You should change jobs if your career is to progress as you want. We only mention this because people have been brainwashed by dogma preached not so many years ago that one should make a career with just one firm, the office-boy-to-president syndrome. Staying in one firm is a philosophy that certainly lowers employee turnover, but at times it is not valid.

YOUR RECORD

Bear in mind that you can never escape your record: it will travel with you everywhere for the rest of your life. Thus you should constantly keep in mind how your record looks to others. When you are contemplating a change in jobs, ask yourself, "How is this going to look to other people when they see it?" In a very real sense, you are trying to develop a good-looking record, one that shows constant improvement and reward for your talents. In the case mentioned previously, Jerry's record had become most unfavorable, for he had made a series of moves downward; any potential employer considering him would not help but be apprehensive. The immediate reaction was, "Something must be wrong with this man. He had a very good job and then took one that was worse." Which brings up a most important principle—your reason for leaving.

YOUR REASON FOR LEAVING
   MUST BE GOOD

There are really only two or three good reasons for changing jobs. The best reason, of course, is if the new position is clearly superior in pay and responsibility. If you leave the vice-presidency of production to accept the presidency of some other company of equal or better stature, no one will question your motivation. This is the best type of move you can make; if your record shows that your changes are clearly upward, you have nothing to worry about. In fact, advancement becomes a strong selling point.

The problem begins when it is unclear whether the move is upward. Then people ask questions. You leave a large company to accept a seemingly better position in a much smaller firm. Did you move up or down? If you took a pay cut, watch out. Although people like to minimize the importance of money, when you can clearly prove that you left for a lot more money, few people will fault you. However, if you left for an insignificant improvement, people suspect other reasons for the move. If you try to sell the bill of goods that you changed jobs for a difference of a thousand dollars or so, you are going to scare off many potential employers, because if you were willing to change allegiances for a pittance then you are likely to do it again. They are not interested in hiring people who think in these terms. If you are going to change jobs for more money, be sure it is for enough more money that nobody is going to think twice about the change.

Sometimes people must change jobs for their health. There are legitimate cases of individuals who develop allergies and can no longer live in a certain area. These are legitimate reasons. Unfortunately, they are seldom believed by others. All too often other people dismiss health reasons as alibis and continue to wonder what the real reason was for the job change.

Obviously there are some bad reasons for leaving, the worst that you do not get along with your boss. If you are leaving because you hate the boss's guts, take care to hide that fact, no matter how right you may be, but that is all beside the point. It never looks good on your record to have been unable to get alaong with someone. Thus your reason for changing jobs should always be positive. The reason should be the attraction of the new position and not the repulsion of the old one.

BARGAINING POWER

Quite early in the job changing process you must make an appraisal of your bargaining power. How strong is your position? How badly does the other company want you? Do they really need you? There are situations when the other firm desperately needs your talents and you are in a very strong bargaining position. In other situations, you have little bargaining power because they do not really need you. They could hire any number of people to do the job. This appraisal is critical to everything that will follow. If you are in a strong bargaining position, make certain that you bargain for everything *before* accepting employment. Once you have accepted a job you lose most of your bargaining power, for they know that there is an understandable reluctance to change jobs immediately and seldom is there any chance of going back to your former employer. So make all bets on the first tee.

YOU ARE HAPPY NOW—EVERYTHING IS FINE

One of the biggest tragedies the author sees is the individual who is really happy with a good job where everything is going fine but the individual is too stupid to know it. Some people seemingly are never happy. They do not realize when they have a good job and that things are going as well as can be expected. If they do not have some troubles, they will dream some up, even go out of their way to make trouble. Incredible, but it happens!

Before you change jobs, do some deep soul-searching about what you have in hand and how happy you really are. This is particularly critical at a certain stage in a career when a person is about to advance into higher echelons of management.

Let me relate the tragic case of Jack, a brilliant young engineer who was doing exactly what he wanted to do. He was a project manager in charge of developing new products. His was a relatively low level management job in a large organization located in a western university town. He had a wife and three boys. Jack was really enjoying life to the hilt. He had his golfing buddies at the country club and was active with his sons in Indian Guides and Little League. He was leading the so-called all-American good life. But then top management took note of Jack. He was too good for his present position, so he was offered a promotion with a nice pay raise, which so flattered Jack's ego that he accepted it. To do otherwise would have been tantamount to the kiss of death in that organization, so Jack moved up a notch. Now he had to spend more time working. He could not spend as much time playing golf and playing with his kids, but their new affluence eased the pain somewhat. Jack was still doing a good job, thus he was given other promotions. It was not long until Jack woke up one day to discover that he was spending no time with his kids, he had not played golf in a year, and he was not happy with anything he was doing. He really did not like his life at all. His marriage was nearly on the rocks, and there was no happiness in his household. Yet he was locked in, for his family living standard was now geared to his high salary. Yes, it was a classic case. It is a damn fortunate person who knows when he is happy and knows how to stay that way. Promotions do not automatically bring happiness unless the promotion is what you really want.

RELOCATION FUNDS

Bargain heavily for monies with which to relocate when you change jobs. Be warned that it always costs far more money to move than you ever dreamed. Many unseen costs eat away at your funds. These costs mount to thousands of dollars, thus do not be deluded into thinking that you can change jobs and move for a minimum of money. Your new employer should pay a generous relocation allowance. Moreover, you need time. It is difficult to understand how executives seem to be able to move from city to city without taking off many days from work. It is difficult to buy a new house inside of a week and yet an executive with the Dow Chemical Company had one day to buy a house. He bought one within two hours. Now that is incredible!

Bargain hard for all these things. If you are not able to get them, bear in mind that any pay increase you are talking about must be reduced by your relocation costs.

TALK TO OTHERS

A person is most fortunate to have a friend or acquaintance wise in the ways of the business world with whom to talk over a job change. Just bouncing everything off someone else and kicking it around can be an immense help. Many times things are put into proper perspective by other people. When the individual keeps everything to himself, he loses perspective. Thus, one should not be reluctant to talk over this matter of changing jobs with confidants.

USE YOUR EYES AND EARS

Investigate new opportunities carefully. This seems so obvious but evidently the advice is needed. Jane accepted employment with a furniture manufacturer, only to be involved in administering the burial of a dead horse. If Jane had taken the time to listen to what people were saying about the furniture company and to examine what was in the factory, she would have quickly seen a company in great financial trouble. The line was unsaleable; things were not moving through the factory right. There was all sorts of evidence about the company's troubles, but Jane was blinded by the title and the promised pay, so she took the bait. You had best learn to look the horse in the mouth. Don't buy into a bankruptcy.

THE BOSS

Possibly the most important thing about the new job will be your new boss. Make no mistake about it, your fortunes in life depend greatly upon how fortunate you are in selecting bosses. Indeed, Richard Irish's book *Go Hire Yourself an Employer,* advanced the thesis that you should be doing the hiring when looking for a job rather than vice versa—a noble attempt at getting across the basic idea that your fortunes very much rest upon your boss. If you select a boss who appreciates your talents, knows how to use your capabilities, develops you, advances your interests, and knows how to run the business, you will indeed be fortunate. If you have basic personality conflicts with your superior, no good will come from them. Discord will work upon you every minute of the day, eating at you and blocking your chances of success.

A young, particularly capable engineer whose services were sought by an acquaintance he had made in a local club, arranged a long trip to a sporting event in which the two men had a mutual interest. They spent more than a week on the adventure, during which time the young man had ample opportunity to discover whether or not he would be able to work for the other man. He decided he could get along with him sufficiently well that there was a basis for a good relationship; thus he accepted the job.

Admittedly, it is a very difficult problem for one to get to know the potential boss very well. If you have the slightest doubt, if you detect things that worry you, by all means dig deeper into the situation, for chances are something is there that will blossom into a full-blown irritant.

A man of some stature in his industry was being interviewed for a key post reporting directly to the president in top management of a large organization. While all seemed to go well in the interview, the man sensed that the two men held different values on some key issues. The president was from the "Flog 'em to let them know who is boss" school of management, while the recruit believed in leadership through close contact with his organization. The man declined the job. There would have been trouble between the two and he knew quite well who would have prevailed.

SHIPS THAT PASS IN THE NIGHT

Business folklore is saturated with cliches about opportunities that rarely rap at one's doorway. Such platitudes usually are well based on experience. Opportunities do have a way of knocking only once. Something that looks like a golden opportunity may come your way and you set it aside with the thought that you can pick it up at a later time if need be. Later, when you go to cash in on that opportunity, you will probably find it has evaporated. Several such opportunities present themselves somewhere along the career paths of most people and if they are not seized, they evaporate. This problem has been thoroughly covered before. One must be able to evaluate these opportunities as real and appropriate for your career path. We only mention this here because many very successful people owe their places in life to the fact that they seized some opportunity at the right time. They took a chance and won.

GO HAVE A LOOK

Go look at a job, even though you do not think you are interested in it. You never know what is there or what will develop from the visit. Joe Jr., an accountant with a large food processing concern, was approached by a smaller canner in Fresno about working as his chief accountant—the company comptrollership. Joe drove up one day to look over the situation. He did not want to move from Los Angeles to Fresno, so he turned down the offer, even though it had many attractive aspects. However, the president of the Fresno cannery was so impressed with Joe's talents that he mentioned Joe to a friend who was president of a large firm in Los Angeles. The net result was that Joe is now comptroller for the Los Angeles company, a very handsome position. The moral of this story is clear. You never really know what will develop from contacts made in influential circles; thus, take every opportunity to explore new situations. Go look at a job, for you never really know what may result.

THINK ABOUT IT

When you are hung up, mired in the middle of a dilemma about changing jobs, do not press it. Do not try to force a decision. Rather, sit back and think about it, preferably at night where you can think and relax by yourself with no distractions. Try to get a perspective of the whole picture. In time you will usually see clearly what you should do.

Paul was a purchasing agent in the Los Angeles area who was being wooed by a food processing company in the Willamette Valley in Oregon. He took a trip to look over the situation and liked what he saw. However, Paul also liked where he was. He had a real dilemma in deciding whether to move his family to Oregon. There were many trade-offs. The job did have more responsibility and the environment was quite pleasant. Paul decided not to go home immediately, but rather to sit and ponder by himself on the Oregon coast for two days. By the end of the two days he saw quite clearly that moving to Oregon would be a mistake. The new position simply did not offer the things that he really wanted.

Terminations—You Resign or Are Fired

It happens! All the time it happens! People quit or are fired. The person who works for only one employer during a lifetime is rare. Much has been written about what to do when you are fired, but the subject is also discussed here for the sake of completeness, for it is very much a part of the management of your career.

First, let us all recognize that terminations have their painful moments. Usually it is not easy to leave an organization for which you have worked for any length of time. You have made many friendships and are comfortably ensconced in the work group. Granted, there are cases where this is simply not so—some people leave with glee, for they have formed few, if any friendships, are not members of the work group, and gladly flee the scene. While the situation of the person who has voluntarily resigned is obviously pleasantly different from someone who has been fired, still many of the problems are the same. Thus, we will discuss both topics at this point.

ABOUT RESIGNING

When one accepts an offer of a better job, one might think that no problems are connected with resigning. Well, surprise! Once you have told the organization of your resignation strange things may start happening to you. In some cases you might begin to think that you have acquired a case of leprosy. You notice that you are being treated differently. Bear in mind that when you resign, in essence, you symbolically reject the work group and the people in it. Psychologically you may be doing something others would like to do but cannot. Thus some jealousy may be involved in their feelings. Or they may be perfectly happy in their work group; thus when you reject it, you are rejecting them and their values. In any case, their relationships and attitudes toward you may change. This point brings up the first bit of advice.

GET OUT QUICK

It is pointless to be a lame duck for it does no one any good; neither you nor your company benefit. As a lame duck, you really cannot do much for the company. You are suspect; your motives are suspect. Once you have quit nobody really expects you to work very hard. Buried deep is the fear that in some manner you are going to rip off the company. Keep your lame-duck status as short as possible and the situation will be more tolerable. If you know that you are going to resign far in advance of your date of separation, you may be wise to keep your departure a secret as long as possible. You may be in for a surprise when your employer tells you he is not willing to carry you as a lame duck: "Get out now! You are of little value to the company now." Naturally, what happens depends upon you, the situation, and your relationship with the firm and your boss, but even the closest and friendliest of relationships have quickly soured when the individual resigned.

Tom found that out the hard way. Tom, a top-flight salesman, had advanced with a manufacturing firm that had grown large. He and the boss were as close as two people can be in such a relationship. They thought the world of one another. Tom was eventually made president of a subsidiary and had led that organization to success. He had an opportunity of becoming president of another, larger firm in which he would own most of the action. After much agonizing and soul-searching he resigned. Granted, there were irritants in his relationship with the parent company gnawing at him, such things as overly restrictive controls, still Tom wanted to be on his own. When he told the old man of his resignation the scene was not pretty. The boss became vindictive and fired him on the spot. To this day the boss insists that he fired Tom; Tom says he quit. There is no love lost between them at this point. The boss even tried to do Tom out of his pension rights.

The closer the relationship, the more hurt there is when one resigns. So do not think that all you have to do is throw down your letter of resignation on the boss's desk and walk out scot-free. Leaving may not be that easy.

HAVE SOME GOOD REASONS

Everyone will want to know why you are quitting. You should have a suitable answer. Seldom does the truth fill the bill. Remember that these matters are usually immensely complex. You could probably sit down and write twenty reasons why you are resigning and twenty more why you should not do so. Resolving all of these, making the necessary trade-offs, can only take place in your head. Finally you reach a decision one way or the other. Explaining the thought processes underlying your resignation becomes exceedingly bothersome. Rather, you need to develop one or two cogent, socially acceptable reasons for quitting, which in our culture are relatively few. Normally, few people will find fault if you are resigning to better yourself—a better position, more pay, more responsibility, or more opportunity. Thus, reasons in this vein are culturally unchallengeable, although some people may doubt your judgment in considering the opportunity an improvement.

Sometimes health can be used as a valid reason, but not always. If a person is suffering from ailments caused by the environment such as severe allergies, life is miserable and that certainly is a valid reason to move. However, there are cynics unwilling to accept one's health as the real reason for resigning; they prefer to see other devils in the deal.

Above all, you should avoid giving reasons that focus on your dissatisfaction with the company or with your situation. These are considered socially unacceptable and may brand you as a malcontent or unable to get along with others. This is regarded in management circles as the most cardinal of sins.

DON'T BURN YOUR BRIDGES

Possibly one of the biggest mistakes the resigning person can make is to regard leaving as an opportunity to tell off the people he does not like, thus enacting the grand scene that one has cherished in one's dreams for many years. Well, keep it in your dreams, for little good can come from venting such emotions. You may feel better for it momentarily, but rest assured that the odds are quite high that you will regret it later. Such scenes have a habit of coming back to haunt you in several ways. First, bear in mind that you never really know what the future holds. You may want to return to that company at some time in the future, thus you ought to leave a bridge standing to recross if the need arises. Second, more likely you will want references from those people. Future employers will be contacting them regarding their opinions of you. Certainly a grand finale is not likely to be productive of good recommendations. Third, word-of-mouth attitudes are simply passed among people in any industry. The people you tell off certainly are not going to admire you for it and they will try to even the score.

Larry was an outstanding young man with a trucking company that had a bright future, but for some reason he chose to go into a larger concern. The boss was deeply hurt, for not only was he fond of Larry, but had done everything in his power to promote Larry's career. He had given him favored treatment at every turn and now felt betrayed. Even more cutting was Larry's spoken venom after he left, accusing the boss all sorts of things. In the jargon of the trade, Larry was bad-mouthing his former boss. That was stupid!

As a general principle, one should never bad-mouth his former employer. Think a minute. It does not make you look any better and in many people's eyes you hurt yourself badly. If you cannot say good things about your former employer, then do not say anything. Particularly, do not go around aggressively forcing your plaints on all who will hear.

WATCH OUT FOR CAUSES

Some of the most useless resignations result when the individual thinks he or she is supporting a cause by resigning. Perhaps my academic background forces me to include this, for it may not be as prevalent in industry, but time and again I see young people hurt their careers badly by resigning from a position not because anything is wrong with their personal situations, but as a matter of principle.

Mary W. was a particularly promising, bright young woman who had joined the faculty of a leading state university. They had given her top dollar and rapid promotions. She was a young woman on the move. She had formed some warm friendships with other young people on the faculty, one in particular, Doug D. When time for promotions and tenure came around for Doug, the administration refused to give him tenure. He was out at the end of the following year, not because he was incompetent or did not know his subject, but because he was hurting the department in enrollments. He was an exceedingly demanding teacher who had the misfortune of also being boring. He could not attract students and the department's budget was being hurt. Beneath the surface was also the hint that he had created a lot of personal animosity toward himself by his continual harangues about raising academic standards in the institution. He was constantly complaining about the low standards of the school, which is another way of saying that he had higher standards than his colleagues. These statements do not sit well with others, thus Doug was out. The decision incensed Mary, for she thought it a grave injustice to her academically respected friend. So Mary immediately resigned to accept a position at a lesser school, and interestingly did the same thing a year later—resigned in protest over a cause—and is now teaching at a much smaller institution. Her career is seemingly on the downgrade.

Usually there is little to gain in resigning to fight a cause. If you really want to fight for a cause, you are much more effective staying in the organization and doing so. Once you have resigned, you have lost your effectiveness completely.

THE STAMPEDE SYNDROME

Situations exist in which several people in an organization are unhappy for some identifiable reason. It is not at all rare that a number of them submit their resignations in rather rapid fashion, perhaps all together in a mass resignation in some sort of protest. Sometimes a key individual to whom others have a great loyalty resigns. Then the stampede is on as others race in with their resignations to follow their esteemed leader. Careers have been trampled into the dust by such stampedes. Many times followers are urged by their peers or superiors who have resigned to join in the exodus, for such people like to promote stampedes; it helps justify what they are doing to the outside world. The malcontent who has been unable to get along with the organization and resigns often speaks of the number of similar resignations that accompanied his, ostensibly for the same reason, thus saying to other people, "Look, what I tell you is true. I was not the only one who quit because of the injustices." Thus, some people resign and set about to encourage others to do likewise. This is a mistake.

Terry was unhappy for a number of reasons. His place in the organization was not what he wanted. When the annual raises were passed out, he received the smallest, slammed it on the desk, and told the boss what he could do with it—the grand scene. Thus Terry exited from the industry. He immediately set about to woo away his entire group. He really tried hard to lure others in his department to follow him. He might have been more successful if he had some definite proposals to make, but Terry had resigned without having a place to go, a terrible mistake. He was unsuccessful in promoting his stampede.

DON'T BE EAGER

In some instances people resign in haste to repent in leisure. No matter how good the other job may look, still you must think things through carefully. Do not be so eager to resign that you rush blindly into something else. There are worse situations, regardless of what you might think at the time. Perhaps Dale's situation is so ridiculous as to be unbelievable, still it illustrates this point.

Dale had a good job with IBM where he was relatively content. However, he encountered a particularly social and persuasive man at a cocktail party who owned a small, peripheral equipment company. The man painted a bright, exciting picture for Dale and offered him the marketing managership of his company, a vice-presidency, at an attractive salary. Dale gave the matter little thought. He knew of the company, inasmuch as it was a competitor, and had heard of the man's reputation for inspirational leadership. Dale accepted, for between the booze and the man's rhetoric, he had become excited beyond words over the career possibilities being offered. He resigned from IBM to accept the job, only to quickly discover that the company was in dire financial straits and was but one jump ahead of the sheriff. The boss wanted a person of Dale's abilities in a desperate hope to save the ship that had an unpluggable hole in the bottom.

YOUR LETTER OF RESIGNATION

The document you present to inform your boss of your resignation is most important, for it goes into the files and you may want to keep a copy for your own records. Here you can show some class. Typically, the letter relates how happy and rewarding your association with the company has been, but that now you have an opportunity to better yourself and feel you should take it, or whatever other acceptable reason you care to use. Your letter is not the place to itemize a list of grievances nor is it the place for a tirade against the boss. Just keep it a short, simple letter, friendly in tone.

SHOW SOME CLASS

The person with class, no matter how he or she really feels about a former employer, does several things to demonstrate savoir faire. Even after resignation he will still put out 100 percent of his effort in the company's in-

---

terests. He is ethical. He does not take the opportunity to rip off the company, taking home everything that is loose. He is helpful in providing the transition for his replacement. There are many little ways to show your ethics. The person with class is not vindictive. Think a minute: why should he be? That the organization has been kind enough to furnish him employment for some period of time is scarcely a reason to throw sand in its face upon leaving.

YOU ARE NOT BEING REJECTED

Many of the toxic attitudes demonstrated by some people who resign are caused by a rather interesting reaction that develops in their thinking. Deep down the person probably did not want to leave the company. Leaving is painful. We would like to stay put and have some stability in our lives. Thus, when we resign we are tempted to feel somewhat bitter toward the employer for "letting us resign." There is a nagging feeling that somehow your former employer should have gotten on his knees and begged you to stay, offering you riches and power as enticements. Well, dream on—it's not gonna happen! Nor should it.

Ron found that out the hard way. He was an accountant, a very good one, but was impatient over many things that seemed wrong in the rather lethargic organization for which he worked. Ron walked into the boss's office one day and slapped down an offer from another firm. The offer was not that much better than what he was making, but it was better. Ron was playing a version of the holdup game, but he did not know his man. The boss stood up, smiled and said, "Well, Ron, I'm sorry to see you go. We valued you very highly and will miss you, but good luck.

So long, it's been good to know you!" This is exactly what most bosses would say in such circumstances. Ron came out of the meeting in a most vindictive mood. He was mad; he had not wanted to resign. He liked his job but had been trying to communicate with his boss by using the resignation as a communications medium but it did not work.

Your resignation is only a good means of communicating to your boss that you are quitting. Your expectations are unrealistic if you harbor the thought that somehow the boss will talk you out of your resignation. This happens only in a small percentage of cases. Think for a moment of the reasons good bosses will not beg you to stay. Once someone intends to resign, if the boss were to entice him to stay by begging and making promises, thereafter how much control would the boss have over the individual? Hasn't the boss created the indispensable person, at least in the subordinate's mind? How are others going to react? Will the boss be seeing a long string of resignations in the hopes that they, too, will be able to obtain similar concessions? As a matter of policy, few bosses care to play this game. Rather, they view individuals as mature people and if such a person resigns they assume he has weighed the decision carefully and has concluded that it is the wisest course of action. Indeed, many would consider it unethical to try to persuade the individual one way or another.

So You've Been Fired

Termination is quite a shock. It ranks high among the shocks one can get in life. No one likes to be rejected, and no matter how well one manages to disguise true feelings,

---

the fact is that when you have been fired you have been grievously hurt. True, you will develop rationalizations as defense mechanisms for protecting your ego, but nevertheless the shock is there. Shock is stressed for it is one key to dealing with this situation. Recognize that the person who has been fired is in severe shock and act accordingly. Do not expect normal behavior from them. Realize that the person is bound not to be normal and deal with him or her accordingly. If you are that person, realize how emotionally upset you are and do not lose your wits. Many people in such situations do irrational things, even commit suicide. They panic and lose their wits over the thought of being fired. Yet it is a common occurrence, and in more than 99 percent of the cases everything comes out all right after some economic loss has been suffered. Sometimes even that does not come to pass, for you may get severance pay and obtain another job immediately. Here is an example of the silly things I have seen people do upon being fired.

Robbie was manager of a computer operation who lost his job in the cutback of 1974. He was fired, not laid off. He immediately bought a $15,000 motor home, put his fine residence on the market, and declared to his family, "We're going to tour the country for a year or two and live on welfare. I'm tired of working." He grew a beard and generally let his appearance degenerate. Finally his wife put her foot down and said, "I'll see you in divorce court first." She took the three kids and started to march. After loafing around home for three months, Robbie finally sobered up and got another job. He did have marketable talents, but while in shock, he simply lost his wits. In a very real sense he had gone crazy. Oh, yes, about the motor home. Robbie was saved from his mobile home foolishness by a bank that would not lend a lot of money to a man who was unemployed. The deal fell through.

Bear in mind that sound judgment is necessary for making wise career decisions. We know that emotion blocks good judgment. Indeed, it seems impossible to have sound judgment when one is emotionally upset. Thus recognize that when you are emotionally upset any judgments you make are almost bound to be wrong. Just do not make decisions under those circumstances; it is another way of saying, "Keep Cool."

THEY SELDOM TELL YOU THE REAL REASONS

One seldom knows the real reason for being fired. Typically the boss wants to hide the reasons by using the terms layoff, cutbacks, or by trying to blame your firing on outside conditions over which neither of you has control. This is a face-saving gambit for the boss, for few people really enjoy firing someone. It is one of the most painful things an executive must do and many bosses are simply not up to it. Thus, most of the time you will not know the real reason for your departure. Far more often the person fired is made to resign through a series of harassments designed to make him or her quit. Again, the truth is hidden.

SUDDENNESS

The really adroit firers do it quickly. Jack was director of communications for a large Southern California company, sitting comfortably at work one afternoon. He was looking out his window at the ocean when a man entered his office, identified himself, and said, "You're being terminated. Gather up your things and be out of your office in ten minutes. Here is your pay and severance."

Bang! Just like that! No warning, no inkling, out of the clear blue sky—fired and told to be out of there in ten minutes. Sounds exceedingly cruel, but there is considerable wisdom behind it. Would any good have come from warning Jack ahead of time of his coming firing? What might this do to him personally, and to his performance on the job? Unless a warning is designed to correct some behavior, it serves little purpose. And what of the ultimatum to leave the office within ten minutes? This goes back to the lame-duck problem. There is no point at all in most situations in having someone stay around after they have been fired. Smart management will have set it up so that someone else immediately takes over the job. Quick and sweet. This sounds so cruel, but then again, perhaps it is not.

BARGAINING

The person being fired often has some bargaining power, particularly if the boss harbors some guilt feelings about the situation. Thus, one should endeavor to strike a bargain, which goes something like this: give me what I want and I will retire gracefully from the scene without protest. It is worth something to many people to have a fired employee go gracefully without a fuss and without recriminations. So one does have some bargaining power, depending upon the situation.

There are things you might want; first, of course, is money. Most important of all—try to get as much severance pay as possible. You need money. No matter how easy you think getting another job is going to be, you are probably going to need funds. So either get money in the form of severance pay immediately or try to have the boss carry you on the payroll for some period of time.

Some highly placed individuals may be carried on the payroll for six months or so while they look for a new job. The more unfair a firing is, the more bargaining power one has. In some cases individuals have been known to go to court over an unjust firing; the threat of litigation certainly is enough to throw a scare into most employers. One never knows how one is going to come out in front of a judge. The bug can crawl in any direction. Thus, one does have some bargaining power. However, smart bosses who have often been through the firing process develop ironclad policies and usually will not bargain.

Thus you may want to bargain for other things, such as an office and time to get a new job. Finding a job when you are unemployed is always more difficult than when you already are working. It is to your advantage to appear to have a position—having an office from which to work and being able to say you are working for such-and-such company. An employer who feels guilty about the situation, and who is friendly, may allow you the use of an office as a front for your benefit until you get other employment.

CAPITALIZE UPON YOUR FIRING

One sound tactic in managerial circles is trying to capitalize on defeat. When you are going to lose, at least extract something from the loss. Winners, in their victories, frequently are willing to throw some scrap to the losers. Thus the smart vanquished try to get as big a scrap as possible thrown their way. Perhaps you can get a glowing recommendation in writing from the person who is firing you. Don't laugh—it happens. People have written numerous silly lies to soothe their consciences. This can be a buffer in the future, for if you have a signed document from the person who is firing you stating that you are a fine, intelligent person who has done excellent work, then he is somewhat blocked from telling other tales about you behind your back later.

Dave was called into the boss's office one hot August morning and informed that he was fired. He successfully executed the following tactic. "That's fine, Mr. Smith. I understand your reasons but if you do just one thing for me I'll depart without making any fuss or trouble. Let me resign and give me a good letter of recommendation." In this case it worked. Think a minute: what did Dave have to lose? All the boss could have done is tell him to get lost, and he had already done that.

Jane was a sales representative who used a company car. If she had to relinquish it, she would be forced to buy one immediately, this putting a crimp in the budget. She bargained for the right to keep using the company car until she caught on somewhere else. She needed a car to get around and find another job. Her boss agreed.

Another aspect of capitalizing on defeat rests in your own mind. You can use your firing as an opportunity for advancement. Suddenly you are presented with an opportunity to do something different. Perhaps you can now move to a new area of the country where you would prefer to live or change occupations and do something you think would be more pleasant. Or perhaps you can pursue intended educational goals. Whatever, it does present an opportunity to accomplish some things that were previously out of reach because you were tied to your job.

YOU WEREN'T FIRED!

Most people go to great lengths trying to prove that they were not fired. Indeed, in many circles, particularly in the higher echelons of business, no one is ever fired—they resign. In essence, the boss says, "Your resignation will be accepted." Thus you are able to get out of a situation gracefully without having the stigma of being fired placed upon your record. This can be important, for many people find it difficult to accept someone who has been fired elsewhere. In our culture there is a lingering thought that anyone who was fired is somehow incompetent, even though this certainly is not true.

SIMULATE—HAVE A PLAN

In military circles good management simulates battle conditions, and thus is better prepared to counter likely enemy action. Similarly, you should give some thought to exactly what you would do, step by step, if you should lose your present job. Suppose you were to go to the office tomorrow morning and the boss says, "You're fired!" What now? What would be the first thing you would do? the second? Think about the possibilities and work up a contingency plan. One of the advantages of such a plan is that in your emotional upset after being fired you can use it as a crutch. You decided upon the plan when you were not emotionally upset. Go to your plan and execute it.

AVOID EMOTIONAL SCENES

You do yourself grave harm by becoming emotional at a firing. Outbursts of anger, shouting, crying, shouts of revenge, all show a lack of class and will only prove to the boss that he is even more correct in firing you than he had previously thought. He certainly will think you are no good for behaving in such a manner. For this reason many executives make certain that one or two other ex-

---

ecutives are present at the meeting with the person being fired. The presence of others tends to restrain the person's emotional behavior and there are witnesses if needed should the person make subsequent false charges.

"GIVE ME A CHANCE"

In some cases an individual who wanted to keep his job was able to do so by pleading with the boss, "Give me one more chance to mend my ways." This appeals to certain people, for most employers want to be fair. If they are convinced that the employee wants to mend his errant ways, they will give him a chance to do so, particularly if it really will not cost the company much money.

"BE HONEST WITH ME"

One young man who sincerely wanted a brilliant business career was unexpectedly fired from his first job. He took it with good grace, but made this request of his boss: "Now I don't want you to think that what I'm going to say is in any way designed to argue with you about your decision. I'm perfectly willing to accept it and look elsewhere for employment, but I do want to develop myself into an effective, productive manager. To do so, I've got to find out what I did wrong here. I plead with you to be candid and honest with me and tell me where I went wrong. What did I do wrong and what must I work at improving?"

Now how in the world is a boss of any substance going to turn down such a plea? If you make it, however, you are obligated to take the criticisms with good grace, without trying to counter them or argue. Once the employer senses that the dialogue is going to develop into an argument, he will simply withdraw from the situation and the conversation will be ended.

What to Do

Now that you are "at liberty," as they say in show business, you have some very practical decisions to make about the future. Others' experiences provide some insight.

DO NOT TAKE A VACATION

Upon being fired many people decide to take the opportunity for an extended vacation to "get their heads straight." They somehow think that sitting on the shore of a lake will resolve their problems. All that happens is that they spend a lot of money and drive themselves crazy with worry and fear. Few problems are solved by sitting by a lake.

GET STARTED LOOKING FOR A JOB— WORK AT IT

The more quickly you start hunting for a job, the better. Finding one is going to take far more time than you had anticipated. Sure, sure, I know—everyone is eager to hire your talents! Somehow employers just do not see it that way. Prepare to be out of work for several months. If you expect to have a new job in a week or a month, when it does not happen you begin to be disillusioned. The soundest mental position is that it will take a year to find another position. If it happens sooner, you are happy, but program yourself for a year and then hope it does not take that long. Naturally, this all depends upon you, your talents, and the situation. Some people can get another job immediately. However, too many people feel they won't have any problem when they actually will have one.

CUT YOUR OVERHEAD IMMEDIATELY

The classic case is the person who loses a high-paying job but feels he or she is immediately going to step into another vice-presidency, making as much within a month or two, so the person continues spending. Well, the job does not materialize and the months drag on with the bank account rapidly evaporating. Don't travel that road! You can never forecast the future. Once your money is spent, it is gone. You can go through a bank account faster than you ever thought imaginable. Cut costs wherever possible. Indeed, restricting your spending can be an opportunity for getting your life back into better financial balance. You may be spending a lot of money on unimportant things. Yes, in serious cases unemployment means drastic action.

Charles was the president of a small company before its owner fired him. He had a $150,000 home in a luxurious section of town and belonged to all the right clubs. He thought he would step into another position immediately but was rudely shocked. After about four months, he realized that he had to sell the house, drop out of the country club, and cut back expenses drastically. He did this, for above all, Charles was a logical and financially responsible person. He and his family moved into a small apartment and his wife went to work in a good job.

Of course, the other side of the problem that makes a person go on spending money is that he does not want to give up everything he has worked so hard for—his home, his clubs, and his contacts. Another job is just around the corner and there is always hope that next week something will turn up. He always has several hot leads to jobs. But the weeks string into months and the bank account depletes. When to cut expenses is a painful decision, but one that must be faced.

ABOUT CHILDREN

I told you about Charles in the previous section; the one thing he did wrong was to continue to spoil his children who were away at expensive private colleges. The reason he sold his house and cut back other expenses was to keep those brats in school. Now those kids are not going to be hurt by dropping out of school for a year or two to work; in fact, they may be better for it. The individual who feels obligated to keep his children in college at the expense of his own financial solvency frankly, in my opinion, is a damn fool. Now we are talking about adult children capable of working. Nothing is wrong with having them share your hardship. Adversity may even help them build some character.

SPOUSE SHOULD TAKE A JOB IF POSSIBLE

Nothing is wrong with a non-working spouse going to work as Charles' wife did, for there is no substitute for income flowing into the household. Yet pride gets in the way. Harry had never let Doris work: "I am the provider for this family." Her role was that of the homemaker. Harry's male ego was severely tested when he was laid off for several months, yet he could not bend. If Doris was working, it meant to him that he was a failure. One of the fortunate fallouts from the women's movement is that the housewife can go to work more readily and no one will give much thought to it.

DON'T WALLOW IN SELF-PITY

Sitting around the house, guzzling beer, and feeling sorry for yourself is easy. Don't do it because it is self-defeating. Nothing good will come of it, and a great deal of evil may emerge. Millions of people have been in the same boat. You are really not in any unique situation; the world has not come to an end. You will find another job, so just get to it. You will have to work at it.

At What Point Do You Drastically Alter Plans?

Possibly one of the most agonizing decisions one must make is to drastically change career plans. A time may arise when it would be folly to continue pursuing a career plan that evidently cannot be realized. This type of situation has several dimensions to consider.

LOWERING EXPECTATIONS

Often individuals are simply unrealistic in their expectations. They are looking for a vice-presidency for which they are not qualified and cannot get the job because other people simply do not feel they are capable. Their expectations are too high. One young MBA graduate searched the market unsuccessfully for a year trying to find the typical entry-level job MBAs seek. He could not get one. The reason was that he was most unimpressive. He had to reevaluate his expectations, a most painful process. Now he is back home pumping gas. Typically, people do not lower their expectations until the absolute financial realities of life hit home—until they are at the end of the road and must accept whatever work they can get. Even then some people resist and continue to harbor delusions. One cannot base a good career management program on unrealistic expectations. Going through all of this is pointless if you are looking for the presidency of General Motors.

CHANGE CAREERS

Probably everyone has wondered at some time whether to change careers. Certainly when you find yourself unemployed, you reach a crossroads at which you can legitimately ask questions about what you should be doing. The defense cutbacks of the early 1970s made many engineers reappraise their desires for more engineering work. Many opted to get out at that point; they had enough instability in the constant layoffs and jumping from one aerospace company to another depending on who had the contract. They wanted something of more substance.

Before making any drastic change in plans you should coldly appraise your chances to reach your goals in a selected career. If those chances do not appear overly bright, then it is certainly reasonable to question whether another career should be pursued. It is time for a career reevaluation. Perhaps out of this reevaluation you will become more convinced than ever that you should continue in your chosen field but pursue it with more vigor, which is what usually happens. But, reaffirming your faith in your career is still a worthwhile project.

Politics

I was a victim of company politics.
The politics were just too much for me.

This old refrain is usually sung by the losers in some organizational dispute. They use the term "politics" as if it were some magical skill possessed by those who succeed but not by the vanquished. Politics may simply be a cop-out the person uses to explain his own ineptness at interpersonal relationships. Politics can be many things. Perhaps the individual perceived that his superiors looked

---

upon other people with more favor: he ascribes his disfavor to politics. Perhaps the boss seems to have more social contact with fellow workers than himself; he calls this politics. Perhaps others seem to be more socially adept at cultivating friendships; he calls this politics.

Nothing is mysterious about so-called corporate politics—it is simply another word for interpersonal relationships. People vary tremendously in their reactions to others. Bosses do have favorites. While we would like to think that such preferences are based solely upon the individual's job productivity and skills, only the most naive person really believes that fairy tale. People are social creatures. Most of the real reasons we do the things we do are because of social forces rather than rational ones. Bosses naturally respond to certain people with more favor than they do to others.

A cynic once remarked, "If you suspect that someone doesn't like you, you're probably right." Some people are particularly adept at currying favor. They know how to entertain and be entertained. This is a fact of life. This is the way people are. Lest it bother you, let us hasten to point out that politics is a dangerous game, one that can easily blow up in the faces of its players. The subordinate who curries favor with superiors, based upon social amenities, may not get the desired results. First, such social relationships have a way of souring over time, particularly after the subordinate comes to rely upon them rather than upon performance. True, up to a point, a manager may overlook some shortcomings in a friend, but after a while the manager becomes angry at being put upon.

When she joined the organization, Harriet made it a point to develop cordial relationships with everyone. Her political orientation did not go unnoticed. Many commented that she was continually out politicking, as she would visit various offices to flatter people. In time Harriet became head of her organizational group. She had no fears, for after all, weren't her political fences well tended? The honeymoon did not last for long. First, it was interesting that most of the people in her group had developed a slight contempt for her obvious political activities. She was just too blatant in her methods and they considered this bad taste. Next, as head, she had to make some unpopular decisions and she tried to do it by appealing to previous loyalties. Her attempts did not work. Her reign was relatively short-lived and considered unsuccessful.

Politics are exceedingly tricky. Just exactly what good politics are and are not is certainly open to debate. Much of what you may think to be good political strategy may ultimately turn out to be ill-advised. On the other hand, it certainly seems true that people have difficulty maintaining and improving their positions if they have not given some attention to their political fences.

Mike was brought in from the outside to head an important charitable foundation. The charge given him by the trustees was to go forth to raise money and pioneer new fields. Mike had great visionary plans and succeeded in attracting people with similar bent who immediately launched some bold ventures. Unfortunately, Mike did not tend to his political fences at home. He held many of his people in contempt and hoped they would leave. Those he did not feel were important, he simply ignored. They could go on with their jobs if they so desired, but he made no effort to get to know them. While he had great plans for his various departments, he failed to place people in charge who were sympathetic to his regime and supportive of his programs. In a tactical blunder that must rank high in the hall of fame of famous blunders, in his desire to reorganize the foundation he appointed a committee of old-timers to make suggestions—let them furnish the rope to hang themselves. Instead, they wove a rope for him. Their only recommendation to the trustees

---

was that Mike should be fired. They generated so much heat that he lost his job. Later he confessed that he should have established communications with everyone in the organization. He was very much a victim of politics, meaning that he did not develop the necessary relationships to operate effectively in an organization of any size.

Mike's experience brings us to the crux of the problem: most people who complain about corporate politics are admitting their lack of skills in personal relationships. They are not able to play the game; if you cannot play the game, you cannot very well expect to win. The essence of the political contract between two people is, "I'll support your efforts if you'll support mine."

This bit of material is so short because one can say little about how to play politics, other than to define it as a matter of interpersonal relationships. One simply cannot expect to have much success in any organization if the people in it are antagonistic toward you. Perhaps they are not bosom buddies nor big supporters, but at least one should seek neutrality, not outright hostility. A superior has to be exceedingly reluctant to promote anyone to a position of responsibility when the people in the organization are hostile to that person, no matter how outstanding his productivity and talents may be. Thus, the purpose of this material is to emphasize that your career is affected by your interpersonal relationships. Many careers flounder simply because the individual is not skilled at building support for them.

C.Y.A.

(Sometimes referred to in indiscreet circles as "Cover Your Ass")

Let us clear the air right now about the ethics involved in the discussion to follow. Essentially deception is in-

---

volved and tactics are designed to evade responsibility for some ill-fated venture or decision—thoughts not publicly acceptable to most people in our society. The discussion should not be considered a declaration of admiration for those who find need for C.Y.A. activities, but rather as an attempt to offer the reader a complete view of career management. It would be a disservice to the reader not to cover this topic just because it is distasteful to some people. This is an aspect of managerial life and for that reason should be considered.

Perhaps the armed services and governmental organizations are the most productive of C.Y.A. activities, for the key to one's longevity, and thus his position, is to never get caught making a blunder. People in civil service organizations, who rise to the top largely because of longevity, quickly learn that as long as they can keep their noses clean and not get blamed for blunders, they will eventually rise to a position of power and prestige. But get caught making a boo-boo and that blemish can thwart an otherwise promising career. Opponents will continually use that indiscretion as a weapon against you. One mistake can be the differentiating factor that rejects you in favor of the person with a spotless record, even though that person is a prize boob.

Make no mistake about it, careers have been totally ruined by one mistake. A prime example, of course, is Watergate. Look at all of the careers that lie absolutely shattered in the dust because of involvement in Watergate. What a terrible tragedy it was for young and old alike. People with tremendous careers were at the top of our society, yet one mistake, one blunder... they tried to C.Y.A., but they didn't quite get things buttoned up. In the corporate ring many other careers similarly lie shattered because of one incident that was not covered properly. Bank presidents have spent time behind bars and lived in poverty thereafter when they failed to cover their actions.

It is difficult to read a business publication without learning of some career ruined when the individual failed to C.Y.A. Admittedly, many times the person tried to C.Y.A. but failed to do so, the Watergate case being the most famous. Cynics admonish the culprits, "They weren't clever enough to get the job done."

While all these are grand scale blunders that one can easily pass off as being far beyond the realm of one's reality, there are still many such blunders at lower echelons that can ruin careers in the same way. A young man just about to receive his Ph.D. was discovered to have plagiarized his thesis and summarily bounced out of the program. His career in the academic world ruined, he disappeared from the scene. You might protest, but he could have C.Y.A.ed that action merely by footnoting and acknowledging the source of his lifted material. He simply did not C.Y.A.

A lieutenant (jg) in the Naval Supply Corps deep-sixed a tremendous volume of electronic parts in the Philippine Sea. (He threw them into the ocean.) Now that behavior might strike you as being fraught with danger and certainly most wasteful of the taxpayers' money, but from that supply officer's viewpoint, it was a needed C.Y.A. activity. During the war he had been a most successful scrounger of supplies for his unit. He had managed to waylay and procure by devious means all sorts of parts and equipment to which he had no official claim. During the chaos that is war, the only thing demanded of him by his commanding officers was that he have the needed goods and he was magnificent at that. But the war was over and now the higher-ups were starting to count bodies and supplies. If he were caught with all of the excess goods to which he was not entitled, he would have been court-martialed and severely punished. He made sure that the stock was exactly what he was supposed to have. Anything that was not on his records went overboard without witnesses—he did it himself.

The same officer was a master of C.Y.A. activities. He successfully avoided censure because of one monumental blunder by involving enough high brass in it that the picture was thoroughly muddled. He had obtained written opinions from his commanding officers on what should be done, and their recommendations were exactly what had caused the blunder. Thus, he had set up a situation in which he was merely following orders. "I was just following my orders, sir," an age-old C.Y.A. ploy. If you do not have orders to cover your blunder, then go get some. Find someone who will give you such orders or approve the action.

If you haven't figured it out by now, the whole idea behind C.Y.A. activities is that under no circumstances should you allow the blame for any blunder to ever rest solely upon your shoulders. When some error is bound to be discovered, then your tactic is to spread the blame as widely as possible among people as high as possible in the organization. Above all, never be the lone fall guy. If you are apt to fall, try to get as much company as you can. Bear in mind that when blunders occur in organizations, the top brass are always looking for someone to blame, even though the blame may lie in themselves. They are looking for fall guys, patsies.

Let's look at a classic C.Y.A. tactic. The president of one division of a large conglomerate was playing hanky-panky with the books. He had instructed the comptroller to keep the books open two weeks after the end of the fiscal period, thus recording more than actual sales. Moreover, he had instructed the comptroller several months previously to stop issuing credit memos giving recognition to returned goods, thus inflating the division's sales. The problem was that the division was not meeting its budget making the head of that division look bad. A vice-president was aware of all of these shenanigans and fearful that if they became known they would reflect upon his career. He wanted to C.Y.A. but he was uncertain about how to do it. Finally he went to a good friend who was also a close friend of the top executive of the conglomerate. He told his friend about the situation and asked for his friend's advice. The friend said he should do nothing, that top management was probably aware of the situation and tacitly approved of it. The C.Y.A. activity had been taken; he could now claim that he sought advice from someone esteemed by the company's top management and had been told to do nothing. He had a reputable outside party who was aware of the situation if the incident ever came up. In other words, he was getting his witnesses lined up. In many C.Y.A. activities it is important to know when trouble is brewing and to line up one's documentation and witnesses ahead of time. Start collecting letters and keep certain people informed of the situation so that when the sky falls you have some evidence to support your contention.

The classic situation is in the armed services where junior officers at times will demand their orders in writing when they are in particular disagreement with their superiors. If you are commanded to do something illegal or something you think is ill-advised, you better request it in writing from your superior. You do not want him playing innocent when the roof caves in on the action. When your superior says, "It's all his fault, I don't know anything about it," you want to be able to say, "That's a lie! Here's your memo!" Wise engineers are careful to get their superiors to initial drawings, contracts, and other official papers showing their approval.

More and more, the wise director of a corporation will have his dissents to corporate actions placed in the minutes of the meeting with his name attached, thus creating evidence in case the directors are sued in some action involving that decision. No longer are directors' rubber stamps automatically approving management in questionable activities. They C.Y.A. by having their dissenting votes placed in the minutes in detail. If the director feels the action is illegal, he should say so.

Two successful business executives on the board of a chemical company met for lunch one day and quickly came to the agreement that they should resign their directorships. As one of them put it, "Bill (the president) is walking too fine a line with the law for our good. Sooner or later he will get into trouble, and there is not enough in it for us to want to be connected with it. We ought to clear out." They did—distinctly a C.Y.A. move. If anything is pitiful, it is to see an individual's reputation tarnished when that person stood no chance for gain out of the action. It was a no-win proposition for them.

A judge's reputation was totally ruined when he allowed himself to become a pawn of a wheeler-dealer promoter whose fortunes crossed with the law. The promoter left town with millions; the judge had to stay behind and face the music. He had failed to C.Y.A.

A small business leader was going to meet with a competitor concerning a matter of high emotional content. Since the situation contained the potential for real trouble the businessman asked a good friend of his, with an excellent reputation, to attend the meeting with him. He wanted a witness—a good one—in court, for the situation had all the makings of a court case.

Sometimes you will want to have witnesses or a recording of what was said in a situation. Few things make other people tell the truth so quickly as when they learn that their conversations have been recorded. Their lies can be quickly discerned. After all, the tapes finally brought the Nixon administration down. A dyed-in-the-wool C.Y.A. expert would never understand how any administration could have possibly allowed those tapes to remain in existence one minute after learning of them, for a standard C.Y.A. activity is to destroy all tangible incriminating evidence. In a situation of "it's your word against mine," it is difficult to be nailed, but hard evidence is something else. Thus the adept C.Y.A.er carefully thinks about the evidence he is creating: letters going into other people's files, letters he puts in his own files, the memos he writes, and what he says in front of other people.

Now it is easy to interpret all of the above as urging deceit, so I must hasten to stress that is not the point at all. The basic tactics can be used just as well to protect a person of solid virtue from innocent, but nevertheless damaging, evidence. Indeed, one might make the case that the out-and-out crook does not leave evidence, whereas the person who is basically innocent of any wrongdoing frequently litters the landscape with evidence that others might regard as incriminating. Think for one minute about the Watergate affair. Wouldn't a skilled criminal have conducted himself much differently? Wouldn't all the evidence have been destroyed right off the bat and the key witnesses in the situation have been unavailable for interrogation? More than one cynic has pointed out that Watergate involved largely a bunch of bunglers unskilled at deception. I am really concerned about innocent people getting caught simply because of their naivete.

Unethical Employer Tactics

Some people are shocked to discover that there are unethical employers. Bosses can do things to you that will definitely harm your career. Thus, you need to be aware of these tactics if you are to protect yourself from them. Let's itemize some of the more common unethical employer tactics.

PICKING YOUR BRAINS,
THEN DISCARDING YOU

One large winery has garnered the reputation of hiring the finest minds available at a fancy price for the sole purpose of learning what they know. Once their brains have been picked, they are fired, thus saving the big salaries. It may be somewhat discomforting to learn that people are able to make a great deal of money simply because they know a few essential things. You make money on what you know. Thus, an employer can hire you, steal your thoughts, and then discard you if the organization has no need for you to actually carry out those ideas. While employment contracts are one way to avoid this trouble, they are difficult to come by and are not available to many people. It is better to look at the turnover in the company. When you see a company hiring a lot of good people, then discharging them, you know what is going on. Look at the company's past performance, its track record.

PIGEONHOLING

Many jobs in any large organization require very special talents. Sally was a marvelous sales trainer who wanted to get into merchandising, but the store management wanted to keep her in sales training because she was doing such a great job. Each time she requested a move, they gave her a pay raise and a bigger title, which, no matter how it was said, boiled down to sales trainer. Sally was pigeonholed. She realized that she was going to remain a sales trainer until the day she died unless she did something drastic. She did—she quit and took a job in merchandising for a competitive store.

Pigeonholing is quite common in highly specialized staff positions where you acquire certain rare skills. Employers do not want to lose those skills, for they cannot replace them. Thus, they have every hope of convincing you to be happy where you are. Sometimes you would be wise to do just that; a pigeonhole may be a very good place to build your nest. It all depends upon your ambition and your talents for satisfying it.

LYING TO YOU

You have been lied to before and you will be lied to again. It is an age-old tactic. One boss was particularly happy with the job Sandy was doing selling merchandise. Sandy did a fantastic job in her territory, but she wanted a promotion. The boss kept saying, "Sandy, we're gonna promote you," but he had no intention of ever promoting Sandy. He wanted Sandy right where she was for Sandy was not needed in management.

You might wonder why employers would lie to an individual under those conditions, when they know that sooner or later the individual will realize the deception and will probably quit. Well, there are two parts to the answer. First, the number of years that can pass before the individual finally wises up to the fact that he is being lied to is amazing. Thus, the employer gains that many years of productivity from the individual. Second, by the time the employee wises up, the opportunity to move may be lost since the employee may be locked into the job. The employer is always hoping to slip by the problem some way. He is stalling for time and a lie is one way of delaying things.

BLOCKING YOUR ADVANCEMENT

Ted was a bright young engineer who went to work in charge of the drafting room for a small electronics concern. He did a fantastic job, but Ted was ambitious and wanted to better himself. He wanted to work on his master's degree in electrical engineering. He wanted to attend trade association meetings. One way or another his employer always found a way to block Ted's participation in such career-advancing activities. He kept Ted's nose to the grindstone. He would not pay for Ted's education nor would he give time off or pay for Ted's attendance at technical meetings. At every turn he blocked Ted's advancement because he wanted him to stay right where he was. Good drafting people are hard to find.

On another level, Leo was an associate professor of advanced years. He had never been promoted to full professor, even though his reputation in the field, his publications, and his teaching performance indicated that he deserved the promotion. Leo's problem had been that his "good friend" Hal, his dean, simply did not like him. He blocked his promotion year after year, and dear old Leo could do nothing about it. He retired an associate professor.

Many such cases are simply a matter of a superior who dislikes a subordinate for some reason and decides to block his advancement. It happens all the time. There is only one thing a person can do about it if the superior is there to stay and that is to clear out. Get out from under that individual either by leaving the company or by applying for work in a different division. Even so, the old adversary may pop up to hurt you at the worst possible time.

ENSLAVEMENT

All the slaves have not been freed. Thousands of people are held in bondage to some of the finest corporations in the land. Their bonds are forged with pension plans, stock options, bonuses, seniority, and other elements. Edna complained, "I hate every day I go to work, but I can't quit. It would cost me $300,000 in the profit-sharing plan if I should quit. I've got to stick it out." She was referring to a famous profit-sharing plan of one of the nation's leading merchandisers. Edna was enslaved.

You may legitimately question the inclusion of this section on unethical employer tactics, for after all, that is a value judgment. And perhaps so! There are other forms of enslavement—company cars, company-furnished housing, devices that make it most expensive and inconvenient for someone to quit the company, never mind their satisfaction with the job.

DISCRIMINATION

At this point there is little need to itemize the many cases of discrimination in business on the basis of sex and age. Not only are such employment practices unethical but they are also illegal.

The age discrimination factor is the underlying reason why your career must maintain a timetable. If you allow yourself to become too old for a job, you will be derailed. Gus was a fairly intelligent salesman doing exceptionally well with an electronic components manufacturer. However, he was bothered by some personnel practices he had observed. He noticed that when some of the fellow salesmen turned fifty, for some reason they left the firm. Evidently the company discriminated against older people, easing them out by one means or another, as they passed through middle age. Gus quickly bailed out, for he simply did not care to work for a company that followed such policies. He was perfectly aware that someday he too, would be fifty years old and he did not care to be treated like the others. How does your firm treat its older people? You may rest assured that it will treat you no differently when your time comes.

OVERHIRING

Some large employers deliberately overhire college graduates each year with the thought that they will sort through, keeping those who survive "boot camp." One oil company kept only one out of five of the graduates it hired. Oh, they did not have to fire the other four; they simply left them pumping gas until they wised up that they were going nowhere. Some firms stockpile people, only to peel them off the moment times get tough. One young man was being held in the labor pool of a large men's apparel manufacturing firm. The recession of 1974 forced them to get rid of their labor pool. The lad had wasted a good deal of his time due to such foolishness.

PART 3

Climbing the Ladder

Where Does the Ladder Lean?

During the recession of 1974 Randy was laid off from his first job after graduating from a leading state university. He had accepted a position as a management trainee with a large men's apparel manufacturer because he thought he would like the menswear business, particularly selling on the road. After Randy had been on the job for two months, the company laid off all management trainees and a number of its sales people in a drastic cutback precipitated by the short recession. Randy received his notification Christmas Eve, 1974. Merry Christmas, Randy.

After a month of interviews, Randy stumbled onto an opportunity to sell women's lingerie for a sales representative, Murray. Murray had put together many lines of women's apparel and had built an organization of nine sales reps to sell the various lines in the five-state south-central region of the country. Murray was an exceptionally good salesman, thus Randy became most enthusiastic about his good fortune in joining Murray's small and cordial organization. After a few weeks' training, Randy hit the road selling seven lines of lingerie in a territory that included everything east of Highway 35 in Texas. To say that Randy encountered difficult and trying situations would be grossly understating the situation. He discovered that none of his lines of lingerie was really dominant in the market and that Murray had no accounts for them in his territory. Randy was going to have to build accounts from scratch and on his own money too, for he was paid a straight 5 percent commission with no drawing account, forcing him to pay his own expenses. One evening, while alone in his motel room contemplating his fortunes, several things finally dawned on Randy. Number One: "Why in the world did I ever think I could be a salesman?" Number Two: "Life on the road is terrible!" Number Three: "Where in damnation is all this going to lead me?"

This discussion will dwell on this latter point. Randy suddenly discovered that the job he accepted was not going to lead him where he wanted to go. If he had been succesful selling lingerie he would have made some money, but that was about it. He was going nowhere in management. He had discovered that the life of a traveling sales rep was not what he wanted. Even if he became a successful lingerie salesman, all he could look forward to was more of what he did not like. Rather embarrassingly, Randy recalled a conversation with one of his professors for whom he had a great deal of respect. His mentor had more than hinted that he had grave reservations about Randy's ability and desire to sell, but Randy had not been listening. Somewhere in Randy's background he had become obsessed with the notion that life on the road was a bowl of cherries, but unless one could go out and conquer the territory one was not apt to amount to much either in marketing or business. Randy was embarrassed by having to quit before he barely started. This might have been avoided if he had merely tried to figure out where the job with Murray was heading.

Before you start climbing the corporate ladder take a look at the top to see where you are going to end up when you get there.

BIG CITY VERSUS SMALL TOWN

As we have continually emphasized throughout this book, the matter of happiness for both you and your family is really the pivotal matter in career management, for one is going to find success rather hollow if it contains unhappiness. Experience clearly indicates that the work environment plays a great role in one's happiness. Quite early in life you should make a decision about where you feel you will most likely find what you are looking for, whether it will most likely be found in a small town, middle-sized city, or a big city. Unquestionably, the lifestyle in each environment is distinctly different. Life in Los Angeles in no way compares to the life one will lead in Newton, Iowa. The two towns might as well be on different planets insofar as the type of life one will lead. You are indeed fortunate if you have already discovered where you should cast your lot.

If you are thinking about joining the home office of a company located in New York City, then it would seem logical to assume that if you are successful with that firm you can reasonably expect to be moved to New York City in the future. If that is not a satisfactory option for you and your family, then you had best think seriously about going to work for that firm. If you work for U.S. Steel, it seems reasonable to expect that you will spend some time in Pittsburgh.

Myra was a young woman eager for a business career who accepted a job with Maytag, only to discover that life in Newton, Iowa, is not the same as life in Los Angeles. She was quickly back in Southern California, crying about the plight of a single girl in a small town. Well, what on earth did she expect? A small town is a small town. If your ladder is aimed toward one, then be advised to consider the nature of the life it will offer you.

I was playing golf one day with David Ray, the former field goal kicker for the Los Angeles Rams, and we were talking about his future. He had clearly decided that his future lay not in Los Angeles; he detested the area. He wanted to return home to Alabama. His plans were to become a lawyer in a small town in Alabama. The big-city life just was not for David. He is indeed fortunate to have discovered that. Others I have encountered are not so fortunate; they spend a large portion of their lives in a town, only to discover that environment is the basic reason for their unhappiness. An MBA from Michigan went to work for Gerber Foods in a very small town that was strongly controlled by one church group. Our young MBA's career did not last long with the company, for the city was unpleasant for him. His lifestyle was incompatible with the social mores of the community. He was simply out of tune and suffered for it.

You should bear in mind that life in a small town provides very little job mobility or perhaps even none, from the practical standpoint of changing jobs from one company to another in the same type of work or position. Douglas was the purchasing agent for a small electronics company in a small town in New Mexico. He was not very adept at his job and soon was asked to accept a lower position in the company. The firm did not fire Douglas, for it recognized some obligation to provide him with employment since there was no other employer in town. Doug was not at all happy with his demotion, but there was little he could really do about it. He was not able to move from the small town, and there were no other employers in the locale. Doug was caught. When you work for a company, particularly the big company in a one-company town, you are pretty much locked into that company. You have lost most of your options.

Life in a small town revolves around people. Your social life involves your fellow townspeople and you have little selection of friends, for there just aren't too many people from whom to choose. Your social contacts are often centered in your work group. In a large city, people are more likely to seek social contacts outside of the work group. Life in the big city is more apt to be event oriented—sports, plays, and other special interest activities. As one executive put it, "In a small town your life is people oriented. In a large city it is action oriented."

OCCUPATIONAL LADDERS

So far we have been talking about geographical ladders that affect the location of your work and the resultant impacts upon your style of living. Occupational ladders also affect your likelihood of promotion and the type of work you will be doing. Perhaps the most extreme, but nevertheless true, example is furnished by Robert, the accountant. After graduating from a large western business school, he worked for one of the big-eight accounting firms for three months. Fall found him enrolled in the MBA program, a victim of the real world. Robert did not seem to understand what accounting was about. "It dawned on me as I looked around the firm and saw all these employees of various ages doing all the accounting work that all I had to look forward to was a life in accounting and I really didn't want to do that. I want to get into management." One has every right to ask what anyone is thinking about who goes into accounting when they are not looking forward to doing accounting work. True, a few accountants make it into management, but most accountants spend their lives doing accounting work.

In the previous section we discussed where you would be living after climbing the corporate ladder. This section will be more concerned about the nature of the work you will be doing, for it changes rung by rung as you climb upward.

Johnny K. was an electrical engineer with impressive graduate degrees from MIT who accepted a job with a large electronics manufacturer. As a junior engineer, he was helping on a project doing what he could and learning a great deal. He enjoyed the work and was learning his profession. In due time he became a senior engineer with more responsibilities. He was feeling good about his work, for he was in the heart of engineering, designing solutions to problems. He worked long hours in the lab, but enjoyed every minute. His dedication rapidly paid off, for he was made a project manager; he was flattered. Now he was moving into management. After a few months, it started dawning on him that the project manager's job was not all engineering. He was introduced to the realm of paperwork, contract negotiations, and supervising other people. But the work was a challenge, so Johnny accepted it. He became an excellent project manager, thus he was promoted to head a small division of the organization. Now he was really into management.

Through a combination of intelligence, diligent work, and a lot of good common sense, Johnny finally was promoted to vice-president of research and development, a most prestigious position. But some things were changing in his life. His family was complaining that he was losing his good humor. He was not having as much fun in life. Suddenly it dawned on him that he was not doing what he liked to do. He was now inundated with paperwork and committee meetings. Oh, how he hated those meetings! His workday was meeting after meeting, and the pity of it all was that their results were most disheartening. Little was accomplished and John was an action man who liked to take a problem and work on it until it was solved. He liked the direct approach. Top management seldom allowed the direct approach. Now twenty

---

years later he was doing work he detested. No longer did he have time for things he enjoyed. John was an unhappy man.

And then there was Paul's case. After getting his Ph.D. in chemistry from Cal Tech, he decided that a career in the academic world would be interesting, so he accepted a professorship at a midwestern university. However, the burdens of teaching beginning chemistry students soon took its toll. Craving advanced research, he accepted a position with a world famous research organization. Outstanding performance was soon rewarded with promotion. Within a few years he headed up the organization, supervising 500 people and was totally enmeshed in managerial problems. However, Paul's case was different, for he had given serious consideration to that first promotion because he recognized that it would take him out of the laboratory. He decided that he would like the challenges of management so he launched a personal development program to become a professional manager of research and the results were outstanding.

The culprit in this matter is our cultural belief that one is a failure unless one is promoted, whereas in fact, there is nothing intrinsically good about a promotion. It may be good or bad, depending upon the individual and the promotion. Each promotion means a different type of work. If that work is not for you, reject the promotion. Unfortunately, in all too many organizations a policy of "up or out" is in effect. The person who rejects a promotion is looked upon as something of a freak by others in the organization and is soon penalized. Life becomes uncomfortable and ultimately the individual may find it necessary to leave the organization. This is most unfortunate. And the matter of money is difficult to overlook.

Promotions usually entail a raise, and few people can turn Santa Claus away. The money can easily help one rationalize the wisdom of accepting the promotion.

Several years ago Professor Peter advanced the *Peter Principle* giving recognition to the problem of advancement. His general thesis stated that a person rises to his level of incompetence. What his principle really involves is that people are taken from jobs at which they are competent and placed in different jobs at which they are either incompetent or simply not interested in doing particularly well. Indeed, a psychiatrist might advance the theory that the person is failing in the new job because he wants to fail. He does not like the job and wants out.

In the sales field we frequently see the phenomenon of the top-flight sales representative who is promoted to sales manager. The firm often loses a good sales producer and gains a bad manager. The very traits making the person a good sales rep often cause his failure as a manager. And usually the top sales rep makes more money than the sales manager so this drive to be promoted to management is not solely a matter of money.

The basic problem is that our culture has exalted management and the manager. Witness the horde of books all dedicated to instructing the reader either how to become a manager or to become a better one. If you don't become a manager certain segments of society consider you less than worthy. Success = Management. Or so it is thought by many. Actually management involves distinctly different work than the people who get the work out. Yet we know that many people are totally unsuited for managerial positions. Either they are no good at managing people or they really don't enjoy it.

The Grass Always Looks Greener

Andrea had been disappointed and rather depressed for some time with her job as manager of one of the programming units for Universal Computing. Time and again she would encounter colleagues working in similar positions with other companies making substantially more than her $22,000 a year, which made her unhappy. Moreover, she was not totally happy with many of the things her company was doing. There were petty policies and rules Andrea didn't like. Parking was difficult to come by and the company's quarters were not as modern as those of its competitors. In short, Andrea was not enthralled with her job at Universal Computing, so she reasoned that she might be happier working elsewhere.

She learned that International Computing was hiring programmers and covertly applied for a position offered her at a slight increase in salary—$24,000 a year. International Computing was housed in a large, modern building with ample parking places and was without many of the petty, restrictive policies to which Andrea objected at Universal. Yes, Andrea felt that she was going to be much happier at International so she accepted the offer. It soon became apparent to Andrea that perhaps she had made a terrible mistake. International was flirting with bankruptcy unbeknownst to outsiders; the insiders naturally were well aware of the company's precarious financial position. Moreover, International's management demanded a great deal of Andrea's time; a 40-hour week had yet to make its appearance at International. Most disturbing to Andrea was the lack of managerial leadership now given her. Many days she was left on her own to do a job about which she knew too little. She needed information from management that was not forthcoming; the manager had other, more pressing problems to solve.

Andrea realized that she had swapped one set of problems for another and, all things considered, she wanted her old set of problems back, for she could live with them more easily. Andrea could not take the insecurity and ambiguities of her new position, thus she was cast again into the labor market looking for another pasture with a brighter colored hue.

REASONS WHY THE GRASS LOOKS GREENER

Just a bit of thought quickly discloses why other jobs usually seem more appealing than the one you have.

1. You, thoroughly familiar with your own job and living with it day in and day out, are well aware of all of its disadvantages. Those disadvantages cause you discomfort you must live with every day. Moreover, it seems to be a general tendency of the human animal to accentuate the negative; that is, we are constantly aware of our problems but seem to be oblivious to all the positive aspects of a situation. The parking may be poor and you cuss it out every day, but the fact that the company is solvent and able to meet its payroll goes unnoticed even when you are cashing your payroll check.

2. There is an old saying that familiarity breeds contempt and there seems to be a bit of that adage in every job situation. We seem to become contemptuous of what we have simply because it is so

familiar and old-hat to us.

3. There is the matter of boredom and our desire for adventure. Old jobs tend to become boring jobs. Many individuals move around simply because they become bored with their jobs, even though they may have an excellent position. For these people the adventure of a new position seems to be irresistible. They want to jump to the other side of the fence just to see what's over there.

AND GREEN GRASS CAN TURN BROWN

Certainly there are instances in which the grass on the other side is not only greener but deeper—it is a better job. So you climb over the fence to graze in the greener pasture. All goes fine for a while but then things change. Perhaps a merger or a change occurs in top management and the new environment is not to your liking. Whatever, there is little you can do about the developments. It could have happened to you on your old job too. The point is not to allow yourself the folly of thinking that a new job is going to be your salvation. Substantial risks are always involved.

CLASSIC BLUNDER

While this topic is covered later in the section on Classic Blunders, still the point needs to be made at this time that changing jobs because the grass looks greener elsewhere is one of the most serious career blunders an individual can make. Tens of thousands of people throughout the nation have left excellent positions with good companies in which they were essentially happy, but failed to realize their good fortune. In the new job they frequently find management different from what they had anticipated or find the company to be financially insecure. Many times they blandly assume they will be successful in the new job, but experience proves otherwise when they fail to meet expectations. There are people competent in the positions they hold, but for some reason prove to be unacceptable or incompetent to hold down the new position. It is indeed a wise person who can see the virtues of his present position and appreciate their true values. It is necessary to one's career well-being to be able to place everything concerning a present job in proper perspective and not be lured from it by false enticements.

MOTIVATION OF THE OTHER PARTY TO MISLEAD

Bear in mind that not all potential employers are honest and aboveboard. Many have ulterior motives, and serious conflicts may arise between your interests and theirs. This is particularly true if you are an able individual with some reputation. In such instances people with shaky enterprises will frequently seek you out in order to use your reputation as a stabilizing influence in their operation.

Fred J. was a promising young CPA who had developed a good reputation in a midwestern city of some 200,000 people. He was fairly well known to the bankers of the community as a man of integrity and capability. Bill W. had a new insurance venture that was in trouble. There had been irregularities and the insurance authorities and bankers had given Bill a few months to get his house in order. Bill enticed Fred into working as comptroller of his insurance company by painting a rosy picture and giving him a financial deal involving options and other emoluments that Fred found difficult to ignore. Fred left his job with the CPA firm to work as comptroller of the insurance company, a decision he would regret each day he lived thereafter, for he became embroiled in a seemingly endless string of lawsuits, both civil and criminal. The insurance company was a fraud and he was made part of that fraud by becoming enmeshed in it. His reputation was permanently tarnished; he suffered financially and professionally, despite his real innocence in the whole affair. His only crime was that of being extremely naive about the true nature of Bill's operation. He had let his greed blind him to Bill's character.

This example is not at all uncommon, for the Bills of the world need the Freds—the honest, upstanding citizens—as a front for their operations and they will seek them out, offering all sorts of enticements. As a matter of fact, they will say or do whatever it takes to get the person, knowing full well that they have no intention of delivering on the promises. Thus, in a very real sense, the more lucrative the offer, the more suspicious one should become.

For some reason, professional sports are most productive of the greener-pastures fallacy, for we see many individuals trapped into unfortunate situations by the enticements of unscrupulous promoters. The real problem here is that the professional athlete is so naive about these matters that he is easy prey. All he considers is the money being offered him, and he is not sufficiently sophisticated to know the difference between money in hand and IOUs. Perhaps the current plans of Ed "Too Tall" Jones, the former Dallas Cowboy defensive end, to become a prize fighter will prove to be a case in point.

CONCLUSION

In conclusion, simply be aware that you will continually see other pastures that appear to be much greener than the one you are presently grazing in, and you'll frequently be bombarded with opportunities to jump the fence. Take care that when you do jump things will be essentially as you anticipated. Be warned that usually they are not.

The Image—Yours

The word image has been bandied about so much in recent years that it is embarrassing to write about such a cliche. Companies worry about their corporate images; product managers try to develop the right images for their products; advertising managers are concerned with image advertising.

Yes, images are phony, but so what? Images are important and that is the way it works. People do patronize companies because of images. They shop at certain stores because the store's image is compatible with their own self-image and they buy products that will enhance their self-image. They participate in certain activities because of the images of those pursuits. Like it or not, everyone projects images to those about them. Note that the term was plural: images, not image. You may project one image to your mate and another to your fellow workers. Even at work you have one image for your peers, another for your subordinates, and still another for your superiors. And these images are crucial to your success. Essentially, the image your superiors have of you, admittedly influenced by the image held of you by your peers and subordinates, determines your success in that

---

organization. Thus, let us dissect this cliche we call image and examine its components.

Factors Affecting Image

The following discussion of the various factors that affect one's image is personally painful, for such discussions can be superficial and counterproductive. Nevertheless, we should examine this creature as accurately as we can.

PHYSICAL CHARACTERISTICS

Most unfortunately, we are judged first by our physical characteristics. The fat person is put down in favor of the all-American physique, be it male or female. Companies sell products worth millions of dollars to people who hope to alter their physical images, but to little avail. The classic Apollo look will take a man much farther than the facial characteristics of someone less fortunate. A study made of the physical characteristics of corporate leaders found them to be significantly taller than the average person. Larger individuals just naturally tend to dominate interpersonal relationships more easily than do their smaller peers. Be advised that the condition of your body vitally affects the image you project to other people.

DRESS

An article on CBS in an issue of *Forbes* says:

Paley himself concedes: 'I have a passion for quality.' The job prospects also knew that they would be judged

---

not only on their administrative and financial skills, but also on their grammar, their clothes and, indeed, even on the way they parted their hair. Paley is notorious for measuring a man by the width of his lapel. The preoccupation with dress is a companywide phenomenon. All of CBS's executives dress with taste, if not always with style; an executive was once sent home to change his Argyle socks.[3]

Clothes are important for they tell much about you. They disclose to others who you think you are and who you want to be. You identify with certain reference groups by your attire. Bankers dress conservatively, while sales reps flash more sporty attire. One study of retail salespeople showed that clerks wearing suits sold 60 percent more merchandise than those who wore sport shirts and slacks. People who are in revolt against whatever bugs them may carefully nurture an unkempt look built around a wardrobe of assorted rags. The essentially colorless individual who would like to project a different image might consider a change in dress as one tactic. The young person seeking a more mature image might effect a more mature way of dressing. It is rather difficult to project an image of affluence by wearing clothes purchased from bargain basement outlets. People who know recognize the clothes for what they are—rags. On the other hand, people of wealth not wishing to project a rich image find dressing down an effective way to do it.

SPEECH

What you say and how you say it greatly affects what other people think of you. If you have careless speech

---

[3]*Forbes,* May 1, 1975, p. 22.

---

habits burdened with regional dialect, the image you project will come forth rather clearly to everyone around you. For example, in some rural areas certain people want to project a "good ole boy" image to other people. To effect the image, they commit unbelievable atrocities on the English language. Admittedly, such an image is an asset in doing business with other "good ole boys."

MANNERS

Your manners and mannerisms tell a great deal about you and most definitely affect how your image looks to others. Rick N. advanced rapidly in business because of his impeccable good manners. Time and again people would comment favorably on Rick's behavior. Many specific incidents occurred where Rick's career was advanced because of some courtesy he had shown an influential person.

POISE

Perhaps poise is the most intangible of the factors we will speak of, for it is difficult to define except that when people have poise, you know they have it, and when people do not have it, that also is apparent. Poise is your demeanor in a social situation—your bearing, how you say things, your attitude, and what you do. The person with poise is relaxed in the social situation, comfortable, self-assured, and secure. The poised person is not running off at the mouth trying to impress everyone with his greatness. Some people attach the word "class" to this concept, but that word has even less focus than poise, for it takes in a great many other things. The poised person is in control of his mind and knows what he is doing at all times. The person with poise does not get drunk or lose control; he is always in control of the situation. Poise implies balance: a person with poise is able to deal with taxing situations with equanimity. However, poise should not be confused with aloofness; the person striving to gain poise will not achieve it by being reserved.

POSSESSIONS

We are judged by the symbols which surround us, our possessions. The noted sociologist, Lloyd Warner, concluded that perhaps one's residence is the single most important thing affecting social class—not only the type of house, but more importantly, its location. Naturally, how you furnish it inside affects the image you project to others. The person whose home is traditional with a heavy accent of Oriental rugs projects an image that is considerably different from one living in contemporary surroundings.

Much has been written about automobiles, and perhaps deservedly so, for they do affect our image. Many people who wanted to attain a sportier image flocked to the various sports cars when they were introduced. You do tell people a good deal about you by what you own.

PERFORMANCE—ACTIONS

While the previous factors have all been rather well-advertised image builders, most regrettably, this one has been given far too little attention, for performance is an important image component. Lisa's image in the business world was one of a can-do variety. She had encountered several bad situations and turned them around successfully. She could produce quick results and this became rather widely known in her industry as her image. In the teaching world people are quickly tagged as being great in the classroom, good researchers, prolific writers, or people looking for somewhere to retire. Such images are based upon performance. Ideally, it behooves you to develop the image of a person who gets the job done.

RECREATION

What you do in your spare time affects your image. Perhaps one reason for the rapid growth of skiing is that it has been considered a high-status, image-building recreational pursuit. Bowling has suffered because of its image as a blue-collar activity. Traditionally, golf and tennis have been image-building activities.

FAMILIES

Warner made a big thing out of family connections determining social class, in that inherited money was much more important than money one earns—a bothersome observation. But this matter of family is much broader than that. Let's take two men, Nick and Paul, working at essentially the same job in the same company.

Nick had been divorced three times and was now living with whomever would have him. His mother and father had been divorced when he was young and he was no longer in contact with them. In short, Nick did not have much of a family. In stark contrast, Paul was the son of a solid local family in the town. He had been married twenty years and had three children; he was as normal as apple pie. Paul benefited from this image at every turn, in spite of the fact that Nick was by far the better business person. Paul was a "good substantial member of the community" or a "good family man." On the other hand, their superiors did not like Nick's lifestyle one bit. The only reason he kept his job was that he outsold Paul two to one. Anything less than that and he would have probably been fired, for theirs were not very tolerant bosses.

Perhaps nowhere is this family image as important as in the case of single people. Some people still choose to believe that if a man passes thirty and is still unmarried something is wrong with him. And pity the poor woman who chooses to remain single and devote her life to a career, for she will be tabbed by some as an old maid or worse. Without question, your family status greatly influences your image.

OCCUPATION

What you do as an individual contributes greatly toward making your image. Visualize two empty bodies that you know nothing about. Then I say, "Body A belongs to an automobile race driver." Now doesn't that conjure up some thoughts about that person? Can you visualize what he looks like? Then I tell you that Body B belongs to a CPA. You have a different image, now haven't you? We have stereotypes for occupations. A sales rep is supposed to be a certain type of individual, a banker another type. We facilitate these images by our behavior, for frequently we role play: we behave as our occupations demand. The sales rep develops a glib line of bull simply because he feels this is what a sales rep ought to do, while the banker assumes a more conservative stance in behavior and dress for the same reason. Thus our role playing accentuates stereotypes.

Changing Image

Now we come to the crux of the matter: can our image be changed? If so, how do we go about changing it? In answer to the first question, yes, many things can alter one's image. Granted, you might be able to do little about certain of your physical characteristics, although some short people do manage to add an inch or two to their height by various devices, and many people are able to significantly influence their images by giving attention to their physical well-being. Simple things such as hair styling and dress can make a big difference.

During the 1960 presidential campaign Richard Nixon was crucified because of TV appearance in the debates with Kennedy. It was said that he looked as if he needed a shave. When the image-builders took over they remedied that defect in future TV appearances. Certainly the way you dress, speak, and behave all are changeable—granted, not easily, but changeable. Even people with the worst speech habits, if they are sufficiently motivated, can be taught entirely different ways of speaking. Certainly, if you have the money, you can select possessions to fit the image you are seeking. Thus, if you are sufficiently motivated you can mold your image into what you would like it to be. But note the key qualifying phrase: if you are sufficiently motivated. Most people do not change because they do not want to change, and that is fine. But if you do desire a change, rest assured that you can do it if you make up your mind to change.

Now, no one said a change was going to happen overnight; you are not going to wave a magic wand and suddenly become a different person. It will take some time to change and you may have to escape your present environment and choose a new one, for people have a way of keeping you pegged in the same hole. That way is more comfortable for them. Once they have you tagged with a certain stereotyped image, you will find it difficult to alter those perceptions.

When we talk about changing your image we meet difficulty, for there is no way I can know how you want to change. Thus, I cannot give you any specific advice. Obviously, changing images requires changing the way you handle the various factors described above. You may change your behavior, the way you dress, how you speak, and the way you look. You should change your performance and actions in whatever manner you feel is compatible with the new image you wish to project. To effect a change in one's image takes work, but it can be done.

Look Like a Winner

"What is a winner?" you may ask. A winner is a person who thinks he or she is a winner. A winner is a person doing what he or she wants to do, accomplishing what he or she wants to accomplish. A winner is not a loser. A winner feels that things are going his or her way.

Perhaps the greatest winner I have ever met is Bob Teller of Newport Beach, California. Every time I see him the conversation starts out something like this: "Boy, oh boy, am I ever lucky! Let me tell you how lucky I am. I'd never thought about it, but here's what happened to me today..." Everything he does seems to turn to gold; he has been successful at everything. He is a winner.

Let me tell you a tale of a winner and a loser, a study of contrasts. Harold is the winner. During our grade school years he often came to school barefooted. His family did not even have a proverbial "pot." Harold did not go to college, but rather chose to be a farm hand. He is now managing some farms in southern Indiana and considers himself very successful. He is a winner. He has a nice

---

family, he is happy in what he does, and he feels fortunate in life. You talk with Harold and you are talking with a winner.

And then there is Penrod. He was from an exceptionally good family, completed his bachelor's at an esteemed institution of higher learning, and went on for a law degree. He became a lawyer, but he has not found what he considers to be success. Everyone in his family is more successful than he is. Penrod is unhappy because he turned out a loser.

Being a winner or a loser is not a matter of what you earn or what you are doing or even what you have accomplished. It is all in your mind—you are a winner if you really believe you are a winner! Now many people would take exception to this and say that while a person may believe he is a winner, all overt evidences may be to the contrary. Well, you resolve that one. I still maintain that if the person *truly* believes he is a winner, he is one.

While this discussion certainly does violence to most people's sense of equity and fair play, some insist that people cannot be divided into two categories: the winners and the losers. Certainly most of us are a balance: sometimes we lose, sometimes we win. The balance between the two is important for few people win all the time and, conversely, few people lose all the time. So essentially we are talking about balance. Some people seem to win sufficiently more than they lose so that they create a winning image, or at least they know how to make it seem so. And that may be getting closer to reality: the so-called winners may just appear to be winners. They say and do the right things. They may not really win more often than the so-called losers, but the loser makes it seem so by his actions.

There is some rationale behind this attitude. In one round-table discussion of the topic, a group concluded that winning might be connected with the individual's ability to perceive the proper thing to do in a situation and then to do it. They conjectured that perhaps the continual loser may lack the perception of knowing how to play the game. Thus winning and losing may depend upon one's perception of how the game is played and one's perception of reality.

Here is a tale about a loser called Rex. He married an exceptionally nice woman who was also somewhat wealthy from her family's money. Rex managed to go through her estate by the time they had left college, for they were married early in their college days. At first his friends thought it rather enjoyable and funny how much money Rex would lose at their weekly poker games, until finally it became embarrassing. They would joke about renting Rex out to other poker games; they were about to put an ad in the paper advertising him for rent—"Rent a Fish." Finally they asked him why he didn't just send the money in and save himself a trip, since he would be broke a half hour after he arrived at the house. He had no card sense whatsoever. In his first job after graduation he unknowingly became involved in a stock swindle that tarnished his reputation rather badly. He personally lost a great deal of money in the matter. Finally he left his family to live with a hippie in the hills and blow grass. Rex was a real loser. He lost on the golf course, he lost at poker games, he lost at work, and he lost at home. The man could not succeed. The basic reason was that Rex was too stupid to know he was playing out of his league. Everything went down the drain. So much for talking about winners and losers. Let's see what you do about it.

Be a Winner

Whether you are a winner or a loser is important, still it may be beside the point. The important thing may be to appear as a winner. Avoid looking like a loser. What does this entail?

First, avoid doing things at which you lose so you do not get a losing habit. Brad had a few outstanding talents, but would never do anything for which he had talent. He insisted on doing things that he could not do well at all. He had delusions of being a track man; day after day he was out running the mile. He never ran it under five minutes. He thought he was a football player but he never got into a game—he was just cannon fodder. He insisted on doing all the things at which he automatically lost.

Most people would argue that Johnny Carson is a winner. But by his own admission, he tried to play golf and was inept at it, so he took up tennis with some respectable degree of skill, which conforms to his winning image. Find out what you do well and then do it. Do not be a loser by attempting things you cannot do. In other words, you become a winner by winning, so find things at which you can win. If you cannot win at something, don't do it!

Second, you are judged by the company you keep. If you insist on being associated with losers, you will likely be considered one. Seek out the company of winners; associate with people who have that reputation.

Third, talk like a winner. Do not go around bad-mouthing yourself by emphasizing your losses or relating how dumb you are. Make other people think you are a winner, even if you have to bend the truth a bit. Why go around advertising that you were wiped out in the stock market?

Fourth, live and behave like a winner. Winners have self-assurance and behave in vastly different ways than do losers. It is amazing to see the differences between the people on a winning team and those on a losing one. I have been closely associated with both and still cannot truly convey the differences. The kids I have known on a great championship team have no doubt that they are going to win every time they go into a game. They walk and talk in ways that reek of self-confidence and they have pride. They enjoy winning and are not embarrassed by it. When Hale Irwin, 1975 and 1979 U.S. Open Golf Champion, was in college he was confident that he would be a winner on the professional tour. Numerous conversations with him during his collegiate years revealed his quiet confidence in many ways.

PART 4

Personality

The Role of Personality In Career Management

Many studies have been made about the reasons people are fired or why one person is more successful than another yet has less talent. These studies almost uniformly come up with the answer of personality differences. People usually fail because of a personality deficiency. When two people of seemingly equal talents are considered for promotion, the decision is usually based on their personalities. Therefore, it seems that we should give considerable thought to personality in contemplating career management. It is rather obvious that personality and success are highly related.

WHAT IS PERSONALITY?

When we talk about personality we're usually referring to a person's behavior in his particular environment. It's really that simple. Your personality is simply how you behave. Of course, that is the overall view. In fact, you behave in thousands of different dimensions in many different environments, thus your total behavior can be factored into thousands of individual characteristics, thus creating a terribly difficult problem to the student of personality.

STUDYING PERSONALITY

Psychologists have been extremely aggressive in studying personality since the inception of their field. Indeed, the study of personality dates back to the dawn of civilization for naturally we are not only greatly interested in ourselves and our own behavior (our own personality)

---

but greatly interested in the personalities of others. Don't you suppose that the early cave man was most interested in assessing the hostility and aggressiveness of an approaching stranger? These would be very important things to know in making a judgment about the approaching stranger. Mistakes in personality evaluations were fatal and they still are!

It would be impossible here to condense the thousands of books written about personality. Yet we know little about it and are constantly revising our understanding. Thus, this discussion will be brief and focus on personality's impact on one's career. However, it is important to understand the difficulty psychologists have had in studying personality for they seldom agree. Many schools of thought exist as to why we do the things we do. Quite early psychologists were fond of developing long lists of personality traits. Seemingly these were characteristics present at birth or that you acquired at a tender age through the conditioning of your environment. But the trait approach encountered some problems. First, semantics is a problem. Suppose we're talking about the trait of aggressiveness. What do we mean by the word *aggressiveness*? We are prisoners of our language. As a personal example, most people describe the author as aggressive. However, that has always puzzled me, for in most social situations I'm rather reticent. Obviously, other people see me differently than I see myself. So the word aggressiveness evidently has different meanings to different people. Thus the first trap we encounter in studying personality traits is the tyranny of words. What do we mean by such words as empathy, responsibility, intelligence, initiative, emotional stability, etc.? The definitions become tedious and of dubious accuracy.

The second problem in studying personality traits is crystallized by the previous personal example. Why would some people consider me aggressive while others think otherwise? Am I aggressive or not? Do I possess the personality trait known as social aggressiveness? The problem here is that the answer depends entirely upon the role I'm playing at the time, thus we get into role theory. A school of thought maintains that a person's personality traits are not fixed and, indeed, may not really exist as such at all. Rather one's personality depends upon how he or she perceives the appropriate behavior for the situation. Thus, the varying perceptions of an individual's personality by other people is neatly explained. Everyone sees you differently because they see you in a different role. You are a different person to different people. Your mother sees you as her beautiful son or daughter and you exhibit a certain behavioral set for her. You may be very polite and on good behavior. On the other hand, people in your play group may have an entirely different view of your personality because you display a different set of behavior patterns in that situation. The role theory of personality has much to recommend it, for it explains how people are truly totally different individuals as they change the roles they play in various groups. As a person changes groups, his or her behavior changes.

Finally, in recent years much research has been done on the self-concept theory of behavior which, in essence, says that you behave in ways that you think will allow you to reach your goals—your self-concepts—how you want to think of yourself and what you want others to think of you. This is related to role theory, you have a different self-concept for every role you play. We will try to combine all of these approaches in discussing personality and the management of your career. But let us caution you that when we enter the field of personality we are wading into deep waters.

Factors Affecting Your Basic Personality

Before we get into the details of how your personality affects your career, first we should point out some factors that determine one's basic behavior at any one time. The factors are: genetic programming, environmental conditioning, internal stimuli, role perception, and self-concept.

GENETIC PROGRAMMING

While some psychologists minimize the role of genetics in determining one's personality, still common sense, supported by other psychological evidence, seems to make it evident that we are all programmed genetically in a way that affects our behavior. For example, it appears that to a significant degree intelligence is genetically inherited and that in turn affects one's personality. A person of slight stature develops a different personality than a physical giant just because of physical attributes. A beautiful person behaves differently than someone not so fortunately blessed. Well, there's not much we can do about our genetic inheritance so it's pointless to deal with it here except to recognize that it's there and that any deficiencies we have inherited will have to be offset by us in other ways.

ENVIRONMENTAL CONDITIONING

Unquestionably, your personality is significantly affected by your experiences. Your environment has conditioned you. Someone who were brought up on the streets behaves differently than the person raised in a protected environment. The offspring of socially adept parents are more apt to be similarly gifted than children who haven't had the opportunity to learn how to behave in social situations. Fortunately, social conditioning need not be indelible. You can change your environment. If your environment does not provide you with the conditioning needed for some career, than a change can avail you of the necessary environmental conditioning. Granted it's not easy to find the right conditioning. A prime example would be a child of the slums who acquires a fine collegiate training by some means, and during the four years develops the behavior required of people wishing to join the upper social classes. But such people have to be most perceptive of unseen and unspoken behavioral cues.

INTERNAL STIMULI

Unquestionably, your health and physical condition greatly affect your behavior. A simplified, but realistic, example is the person who has mismanaged the previous evening and suffers the physical consequences the next morning—the idiot is hungover. This plight will affect his condition and personality throughout the day. Poor health manifests itself in one's behavior. It is difficult to be sociable and in good humor when suffering. Thus, one's physical condition directly relates to personality.

ROLE PERCEPTION

We perceive the role we should be playing in a situation at any one time. Perhaps it is the role of the dutiful husband or wife or child, or the loyal, hard-working, talented employee. Perhaps it's the good time Charlie or whatever, but we play many roles each day. Success in life depends upon how accurately a person perceives the correct role at the time and how well he or she plays it. Careers have been ruined when people misperceive their appropriate roles. When someone chooses to play the court jester at the office when the boss is looking for someone to play the role of the serious-minded, highly productive employee, not much good will come from jesting. One of the unfortunate dilemmas facing the person seeking a doctorate is caused when they also instruct in the classroom. The question arises: are they teachers or are they students? In the classroom they can play the role of the teacher; that's the role they are supposed to play. But when they're dealing with the faculty guiding them through their doctoral programs, they are students, not colleagues. One unfortunate chap never could get those roles straight. In his relationships with senior professors he never saw himself as a student, only as a colleague of equal status. They flunked him for he just didn't know what role to play. He couldn't get it through his head that a doctoral student behaves differently than a faculty member. How do you address your thesis advisor: do you call him Dr. so-and-so, or do you call him by his first name? This unfortunate individual insisted on calling the faculty by their first names and alienated a few of the more uptight faculty members. He was all too familiar with people as if he was a close personal friend. Many faculty members simply don't believe in being that close to their students. You might say, "Well, that's the academic world, it doesn't apply in business." It most certainly does.

You have to perceive the precise role your boss wants you to play. Some bosses are very uptight and insist on being addressed as Mr. or Ms. and will rebel at any attempt to be familiar or to talk with them on an equal basis. Other bosses want you to play a different role. Your success on the job depends very much on how accurately you perceive the role the boss wants you to play, and your skill in playing it.

Self-Concepts

From all of your experiences you develop a complex set of concepts about yourself: who you are, what you are, what you want to be, who you want to be, what you believe other people think of you and your talents, and what you want other people to think of you.

COMPONENTS OF ONE'S SELF-CONCEPTS

One's self-concept is not a simple, single, psychological phenomenon easily explained or understood. Instead, at least four main components must be studied: the *Real Self*, the *Ideal Self*, the *Real Other*, and the *Ideal Other*.

The Real Self   The Real Self is the self one really perceives, what one really thinks of himself. It is the person's concept of his abilities, personality, character, interests, and values that make up his total existence. This *Real Self* is terribly important to the individual, even crucially so, for it has been well established that if one thinks well of himself he is apt to lead a happy, well-adjusted life. People desperately want to think well of themselves but more than wishful thinking will affect the *Real Self,* for deeds are needed. Admittedly, many individuals fail to accurately perceive the reality of their being, usually with unfortunate social consequences. Witness the joke-telling bore who really thinks he is the life of the party, the "star" who isn't, or the "vamp" who can't.

Some people genuinely do not really know who or what they are. This is particularly true of people lacking sufficient experience in life to find out. Thus, the older one becomes and the more exposure to life one has, the more evidence one has accumulated to fill out his *Real Self*.

The Ideal Self　The Ideal Self is how one would like to think of himself—his personal goal. Much of his behavior is directed toward making his *Real Self* coincide with his *Ideal Self*. One small portion of a man's *Ideal Self* might aspire to be a great football player. His *Real Self* proclaims him to be only average but his *Ideal Self* would drive him to perfect his football skills and participate in the game with extreme vigor. However, the man whose *Ideal Self* wants only to be an average player would not behave in a similar manner. The *Ideal Self* changes with experience. At one time a person might strive to be a great athlete, but change his goal for one reason or another.

The Real Other　The Real Other is how one perceives other people's views of him, what other people think of him, his abilities, and his personality. Notice that this is not how other people actually do see the individual: one's *Real Other* may be far out of tune with reality. He may believe that other people think of him as a social lion while in reality they see him as an utter bore. The entire self-concept theory is based on how the individual perceives himself and what he thinks others think of him.

The Ideal Other　The Ideal Other is how one wants other people to think of him. A woman may want others to think that she is a good wife, a kind mother, and a wise homemaker; she will buy many things to create this impression among the members of her reference groups. Or she may want others to see her as a businesswoman so she will exhibit different behaviors to effect that image.

IMPACT UPON BEHAVIOR

People express themselves through the goods and services they buy as well as through nonconsumptive activities. However, it should be pointed out that extremely few activities in this society do not require the consumption of something. The individual is constantly trying to bring his *Real Self* and *Ideal Self* closer together and to make the *Real Other* and *Ideal Other* coincide. However, one does not necessarily try to make his *Ideal Self* and *Ideal Other* coincide in all respects. A man might wish others to think of him as honest, but he really has in his *Ideal Self* the thought of being adept at sharp practices. Much hypocrisy can separate one's *Ideal Self* and *Ideal Other*.

Think of the impact upon one's self-concept of driving a new Continental. What is the person trying to say to himself and to others? Wouldn't he receive as much satisfaction from it even if others did not know of his ownership—frequently the situation in very large cities. Think of the effect upon a woman's self-concepts as she lolls around a luxurious home among her fine furnishings even though few people may be aware of her fortunate situation. All of these tangible symbols reinforce her self-concepts. Of course, when a purchase affects the *Real Other* also, then far more satisfaction is obtained. But the point is that many seemingly ostentatious purchases are made partly for purposes other than impressing other people. A wealthy man may buy expensive silk undergarments solely for the effect on his *Real Self:* they constantly remind him that he is a highly successful man.

The key point to realize is that the mind continually requires evidence of who and what it is. It is insufficient to be highly successful if there is little or no visible evidence of success. Thus the need for status symbols arises.

People constantly tell the world who and what they are by the various things they buy and do. The college student shouts his status to all through his clothes, speech, and other less subtle forms of behavior. He clearly wants to make certain that he is not confused with a high school student or with a workman of his own age. Similarly, members of the motorcycle set clearly proclaim their allegiances. This symbolic communication is not in the least foolish; it serves as a silent but speedy means of communication. Walk into most offices and the boss's status is quite apparent by the surrounding symbols.

BEHAVIOR AND SELF-CONCEPTS

One's self-concepts are not fixed rather they constantly change with experiences and changes in attitudes, philosophies, and goals. It is a heartwarming experience to observe a young person in the process of upgrading his *Ideal Self*. Perhaps a series of unfortunate academic selections has forced him to conclude that he is a mediocre student at best; his *Ideal Self* requires only that he graduate from college. Then he encounters an appealing subject and his interest and grades soar. At the same time the upgrading of his *Ideal Self* becomes perceptible. He may start thinking of graduate school. He starts acting like a scholar instead of a playboy; he wants to alter his *Real* and *Ideal Other*. His consumption habits may also change; he may even rashly buy some books.

Presently the women's movement is altering the self-concepts of most women and testing the self-concepts of the rest. Women now see themselves differently and want others to see them in a different light. Interestingly, the women's movement is also changing male self-concepts in many ways.

Let's examine some practical examples of self-concept theory in action. Ask most college seniors in the nation's business schools and they will tell you that they want to advance into management. Many, if not most, would be happier and more successful staying out of management. But society has placed the manager on a pedestal, which somehow is translated into, "If you aren't a manager, you're a failure." What nonsense! Hordes of people hold relatively meaningless managerial jobs who would be happier and making more of a contribution if they were creating something. Many professors who become deans, doctors who become hospital administrators, salespeople who become sales managers, and chemists who become research directors can attest to this truth. One basic reason an individual may aspire to a career that will lead to personal unhappiness is that we tend to let our *Ideal Other* concepts overrule our *Ideal Self* concepts.

It is more important to many people what others think of them than what they think of themselves. They will go through life in a career that they personally hate just to satisfy their *Real* and *Ideal Other* self-concepts.

On the other hand, the downgrading of one's self-concepts is an extremely painful process; morale suffers, attitudes degenerate, and one resists the process vigorously to the extent that one can become completely separated from reality. Not only do people resist the downgrading of their self-concepts, but they will resist anything that might threaten them. Anything or anyone who in any way threatens one's self-concepts will be shunned. The makers of games learned long ago that people will not buy games they cannot beat. The customer wants to win; make him a winner and you have made him a customer.

THE ROLE OF REFERENCE GROUPS

Reference group theory is extremely important to motivational analysis. The individual has certain key reference groups from which he takes most of his behavior cues. He conforms to the behavior patterns dictated by these reference groups because he wishes to be accepted by their members. Hence, his *Ideal Self* and *Ideal Other* are largely determined by the characteristics demanded by the reference groups. As a person changes reference groups, the effect upon his *Ideal* self-concept will be immediately apparent. Since an individual usually belongs to several reference groups, an accurate analysis of his self-concepts must develop separate *Real Other* and *Ideal Other* concepts for each reference group. Thus a young man's *Real Family Other* and *Ideal Family Other* probably differs considerably from his *Real Schoolmate Other* and his *Ideal Schoolmate Other*. Note the line at the barber shop prior to the end of a school term as many young men wish to alter their appearance before going home.

Now you are probably wondering what this all has got to do with your career management. Well, all of your behavior in your career management endeavors will be determined by your self-concepts. You will opt for certain careers because they are compatible with your self-concepts and will make your *Reals* come closer to your *Ideals*. You will shun certain careers because they are incompatible with your self-concepts and will not likely advance you closer to your *Ideals*.

But it isn't that simple. Some complexities are inserted in real life. You might like to earn the money of a top-flight industrial sales rep, but your peers and family would all look down on you as a "mere peddler." Your family and others might think highly of you if you worked in a bank, but your *Real* and *Ideal Self* reject that calling. Life is full of such conflicts because one's self-concepts are not harmonious with each other, and often are in total conflict. Satisfy one self-concept and you dissatisfy another. It's the old adage in action, "You can't be all things to all people."

Make some choices that are based on the concepts most important to you. The resolution of such conflicts is so complex that it is beyond writing about. Each person fights them out internally, weighing the factors involved in each instance. The important thing to realize here is that your self-concepts are the very heart of your existence and that the career you choose and the actions you take to pursue it must be compatible with your self-concepts. You will quickly regret taking a job that is incompatible with your most important self-concepts.

Personality Requirements for Various Careers

Now let's get down to applying personality factors to your career planning. By now you should have noticed that various careers have differing personality requirements. One might not be too surprised if an actor or actress was emotionally immature or unstable, but such behavior would be disastrous for an airline pilot or a law enforcement officer. Certainly, the work habits of an accountant and a salesperson are different. The accountant had damn well better like detail work and few salespeople do.

An example of how personality factors affected an individual's career planning is provided by Paul, who from an early age knew he wanted to be a physician. Paul was an exceedingly bright youngster who graduated from med school at the top of his class. We were close friends in our childhood years. Even in high school he had clearly identified that he would go into pathology because he didn't feel he'd be any good at dealing with patients. He felt that his bedside manner would be lacking. On the surface it did not seem like Paul had very many social skills for he had few friends. He found it difficult to talk with other people. They just didn't have much to say that he was interested in hearing, and they were not much interested in the things he wanted to talk about. Paul is a leading pathologist today.

Now this example is not given as a correct self-assessment by Paul, for I believe that Paul was overly harsh on himself. He would have made a fine doctor in many other specialties, for his serious demeanor and intelligence would inspire confidence in patients. I only provide the example as an illustration of how one intelligent person applied his personality assessment to making a career decision and formulating his career plan on it. However, Paul's selection of pathology as a career goal, based upon his assessment of his personality and the personality requirements of the pathologist specialty, is an example of how one's plans can be based upon mythology. Paul was victim of some myths about the personality requirements for various types of doctors.

These myths are widespread about most careers. For example, people commonly believe that a person must be extremely glib to sell and this is simply not so. The person who talks too well is apt to talk too much, and selling requires more listening than talking. The art of selling is the art of asking the right questions and getting the other person to talk. Thus we fall victim to two forces: our own misperceptions about our personality and our misperceptions about the personality requirements of an intended career. We must diligently examine both sides of this equation. A dear friend of mine refused to study for his doctorate because deep down he believed that in order to obtain a doctorate one had to be a true scholar in the traditional sense of the word. He has since learned the error of his opinion, but it's too late for him to do anything about it.

While you should talk with many people in your chosen career about its personality requirements, be very leery of believing too much of what you hear, for many people like to propagate folklore. Instead, you would be better advised to make actual personality observations of people following those careers and to judge for yourself. In other words, don't believe what they say, believe what they are.

In appraising your own personality, be leery of listening to other people, for they may have great misperceptions, not only about you but about the nature of the job. This is a particularly sensitive point to the author, for while in school one of my professors declared that I should never seek a career in teaching for I was "too impatient with mediocrity." Well, I've been teaching successfully for thirty years with high teacher ratings. One reason that I paid no attention to this professor's evaluation was that he was such a terrible teacher himself and I was not going to listen to some bozo sadly lacking in teaching skills. The problem with that professor's evaluation, in retrospect, is that no correlation exists between one's patience with mediocrity and teaching ability.

The moral of this story is that you should be very wary of letting other people make your career decisions for you based upon their perceptions of your personality and the job's requirements. There is garbage that you just don't want to listen to. Moreover, what other people tell you is not always for your benefit, but rather is apt to satisfy their ulterior motives. Perhaps the other person is trying to guide you into some career because of their own interests. Unfortunately, all too much of this happens on college campuses. Some naive student comes under a spell of some professor who is seeking more students to justify his position, thus the professor tells the individual that he or she is ideally suited for a career in the professor's area. This is called proselytizing. Of course, it's all a lot of garbage. The selection of your career is far too serious a matter to place in the hands of other people. You must learn to trust yourself more than you trust others. Not only can you not trust their motivations, you can't trust their judgments. If you fail at something, at least do so because of your own bad judgment, not someone else's.

Can You Change Your Personality?

Many people believe that, by and large, there's little you can do to change your personality. I don't believe a word of it. You can change your personality if you want to. The reason people don't change their personalities is that they don't want to. They are perfectly happy the way they are. Their personalities work for them and get them what they want, granted often times in perverse ways. I submit as key evidence the role playing concept of behavior. If we can't change our personality, then why are we so many different people at different times? It's absurd to think you don't change your personality, for we behave differently at home and on the job than we do at a ball game. We continually change our personality depending upon the roles we're playing. If you want to change your personality, simply play a different role. We do it all the time. The key is to learn to stay in the desired role and not shift into an unwanted role.

We see this in sales work all the time. Off stage the sales manager could not understand how some sales rep with a seemingly colorless personality was described by a customer as a live wire. But once the manager saw the rep at work, it all became clear. The guy went on stage; he came alive. We see this same "stage" personality phenomenon in teaching; the student changes personality upon entering the classroom. He dies!

Don't for an instant accept the garbage that you can't change your personality. The people who insist that you can't change your personality are trying to defend their reasons for not changing their personality. It's their defense mechanism. We must remember that we all perceive certain inadequacies in our personalities but we live with them for one reason or another, and even nurture them at times. We don't want to give up our vices and weaknesses, for we enjoy them. The person who throws temper tantrums does not want to change for he or she enjoys this behavior. They enjoy intimidating the people around them—"You'd better not mess with Charlie over there for he's got quite a temper." Such personality behavior is a mechanism that people have learned to use to intimidate other people and since they don't want to give it up, they hang on to such personality defects.

Personality Factors

In a very broad way let's talk about some of the personality factors that affect one's success in various careers.

These factors are grouped under seven major headings:

Intelligence
People skills
Drive
Emotions
Work habits
Physical attributes
Character

While trying to avoid over-reliance on the trait approach to personality, still it will be very difficult to avoid labeling many of these attributes as personality traits. One of the enticing aspects of the personality trait school of thought is that it is so easy to talk about. Within each of these broad categories lie many more specific personality characteristics.

INTELLIGENCE

Most psychologists prefer to begin the study of personality with an analysis of intelligence, for it seems to form the basic foundation for the human experience. For many years psychologists felt that they really had a good handle on measuring intelligence and knew what it was. However, they have grown wiser and have come to realize that even intelligence is a difficult behavioral characteristic to pin down. Where they once thought they could measure abstract intelligence rather accurately with their so-called I.Q. tests, now they're not quite certain what these tests are measuring.

There are several types of intelligence. First, there is *abstract intelligence*—the ability to perceive and comprehend abstract thoughts. The person well endowed with abstract intelligence quickly grasps the meanings of symbols and the relationships between things in the environment. They can handle math and vocabulary, the symbols we call numbers and words, with great skill. They do well on I.Q. tests because such instruments are heavily loaded with math and language skills. Certainly abstract intelligence is important, but not nearly as important to success in most careers as many people would have you believe. Indeed, even those professions which highly prize abstract intelligence, such as law, medicine, engineering, science, and education have proven time and again that people with a modest I.Q. can still do well. Granted, people with high abstract intelligence, all other things being equal, do have a big advantage in those professions. Fortunately, or unfortunately, depending upon your viewpoint, all other things are never equal. Often people with very high abstract intelligence lack other important behavioral characteristics, which nullifies the advantages they might gain because of their high I.Qs.

In many careers we've come to realize that social intelligence is far more important to success than abstract intelligence. *Social intelligence* is one's ability to perceive the proper thing to say and do in a social situation. Successful people know how to deal with other people; some people have the knack of making other people like them by doing and saying the right things. Then there are people who seem to walk around on one foot with the other implanted in their mouth. Given the opportunity, they can be counted on to say or do the wrong thing in social situations. These people often have a difficult time being successful in careers requiring relationships with other people.

And there's *mechanical intelligence* that makes some people wizards at dealing with things because they know how to manipulate matter. They can build wondrous machines. Often they are poor in people relationships and do not measure high in abstract intelligence, but they have a knack for dealing with inanimate objects. Many of our famous inventors such as Edison, Ford, Bell, and Whitney would fit this model quite well.

Buried somewhere in these various intelligences is that priceless ingredient—the ability to learn. Some people are quick learners whereas others are almost totally uncoachable. Now don't jump to the conclusion that this ability to learn is automatically highly correlated with abstract intelligence, for it isn't. Many people with great intelligence are also very uncoachable. Conversely, some people with very modest I.Qs. are still what is referred to in the theater as "quick studies." Show them something once and they have it. Stress is placed on this ability to learn for it is possibly the most important attribute for a successful career. In order to be successful you have a great deal to learn in any job, so if you learn easily and quickly, obviously you will progress much faster than if you are slow to grasp what must be learned. Unfortunately some people are so totally uncoachable that they are failures. They just can't learn how to do the job.

If an employer asks you to list some of your more valuable personal attributes, it might be wise to emphasize that you learn quickly and are quite coachable. Most managers understand the importance of this so the fact that you recognize its importance will likely impress them favorably.

PEOPLE SKILLS

Under this broad category of behavioral characteristics—dealing with other people—falls a multitude of traits such as sociability, good humor, empathy, and other such words that describe one's ability to get along with and successfully work with other people, toward reaching whatever goal is sought. In business, people skills are highly prized. The person skilled at getting along with other people, who is well-liked, often goes far in spite of being woefully inadequate in other areas. Numerous cases can be cited of people reaching the very pinnacle of success solely because of people skills even though they were unfortunately deficient in other necessary skills. Often these people, who lack basic intelligence or knowledge, have difficulty once they achieve success, having gotten there on the basis of their popularity. Nevertheless they are successful when other people of tremendous talent languish unnoticed because of a lack of people skills. This phenomenon does not happen by chance.

Often people who recognize that they have very modest intelligence and lack other skills realize early in life that their success depends on their ability to get along with other people. Thus, they work harder to develop their people skills early for they found that this is the best way for them to compete in society. The person with great intellect or other talents is often able to achieve goals through sheer talent and ignores the development of people skills. Their attitude often is, "Who needs them? I'm able to achieve my objectives without bothering with people." And often such people do achieve their goals in spite of inadequate people skills. But the road is more difficult for them than necessary.

DRIVE

An individual's drive refers to such things as energy levels, motivation, initiative, mental toughness or determination, persistence, and even hostility. These behavior traits drive the individual toward goals. It should come as no surprise that some people are highly driven while others are hardly driven. Certainly success in any endeavor requires a certain amount of drive. You must have some energy and be motivated or nothing advantageous is going to happen. Some careers take a great deal of mental toughness, that is, determination to reach your goal. Often a frightful price must be paid for success in a career, such as in the area of professional sports. Even the professional pays a rather substantial price in terms of required schooling and apprenticeship.

Often people simply aren't sufficiently motivated to reach their goals that they're willing to pay the price. One of the author's pet peeves is the young person who simply cannot understand why he can't have the same standard of living as I do at age fifty-three. It does little good to explain that when I was his age I was doing even worse financially than he was. In my industry you must pay a price: you must starve while you're in graduate school getting your Ph.D. And the financial rewards early in a teaching career are not particularly handsome, but I knew that before I chose the profession and I paid the price to achieve what I sought. Many people are leaving my profession today simply because they're unwilling to pay the price. They are unable to see the rewards awaiting them down the road or are too impatient to wait for them.

The matter of initiative needs some special mention, for in some careers it's important to be a self-starter. The sales representative who is not a self-starter will not know success. People going into business for themselves must have a tremendous amount of initiative because nobody is going to check to see what hours they work or if they get the tasks done that need doing that day.

EMOTIONS

The category of emotions includes such behavioral characteristics as stability and emotional maturity. In many careers it is extremely important that the individual have good emotional control. An example would be law enforcement officers who must continually work in emotionally explosive situations. They must be able to keep their heads when everyone around them is losing theirs. It's a matter of everyone's life and death that the officer have a good handle on his emotions. Many other careers demand similar emotional stability. For example, lawyers usually must have exceptional emotional control and maturity to deal with the emotionally sensitive issues before them.

WORK HABITS

This category of behavioral characteristics includes the capability for detailed work, orderliness, punctuality, thoroughness, and ability to complete a job undertaken. Quite obviously all of these characteristics are critical to a wide range of jobs, particularly in business. Business has few places to hide for the individual who does not have good work habits. Indeed, many people have been successful largely because they have developed an excellent set of work habits early in life. They were taught to be punctual, to be orderly, to be thorough, and to complete the job. They had a good upbringing. The slob is shunned by most employers.

PHYSICAL ATTRIBUTES

Personality, or behavior, is strongly affected by physical attributes such as personal appearance, health, size, and general stature. One of the most frustrating problems that I routinely face in this area is the tremendous number of fairly able high school basketball players who seek scholarships for basketball in college and hope for a professional career. I remember a charming conversation I had with a young sailor who was a member of the crew of U.S.S. Saratoga that was in port in Malaga, Spain. We met in an Orange Julius stand where we'd sought refuge from the rain. He quickly struck up a conversation with me but only because I had along my twenty-one-year-old daughter. Upon learning my profession he immediately wanted to know the chances of getting a basketball scholarship at SMU. I asked him how tall he was and when he told me he was 5'9", I told him the chances were nil. He was most adept verbally so he began trying to convince me of his talents at playmaking. I'm quite certain he thinks he's the best playmaking guard in the history of basketball. Unfortunately a great many playmaking guards stand 6'4" and even 6'8", and today, in basketball, anyone shorter than 6'4" hasn't much of a chance at success. There will be a few exceptions every now and then but that's not the way to bet your money.

You may think this is an exceptional illustration irrelevant to business but there are physical requirements for many jobs. Did you ever think about a problem that a very large individual, with hands the size of a catcher's mitt, would have being a dentist? I'm afraid he'd have a difficult time working inside of people's mouths. Even in the field of selling it's been established that large people have an advantage over small individuals because they're better able to dominate the scene, since the large person is not intimidated as easily and other people are not likely to try to intimidate them.

CHARACTER

While some people could argue that the words character and personality could be considered synonyms, I've used

---

character here for want of a better word to describe such behavioral characteristics as honesty, responsibility, and integrity.

Certainly these traits are all very important in most careers but in some callings it's absolutely necessary that a person have impeccable integrity and honesty if he or she is to realize success. The person tainted with a record is not apt to go far in the financial community. A criminal record would keep one from enjoying law and other professions. (On the other hand, if you wanted to be an umpire . . .)

CONCLUSION

Little more can really be said about the relationship of personality and career selection. Only you can make this decision, for the demands of each career are unique and only you are able to pin down your behavioral characteristics and relate them to the needs of that career. The sole purpose of this section was to stimulate you to think about these considerations.

PART 5

Women
in
Business

Women in Business

Since the first edition of this book was published, one of the truly significant developments in business has been the highly increased interest among women in business careers. Since many articles and books have been written on the subject of women in business, there is little need to repeat the material in those publications, which, by and large, is most useful to the woman contemplating a career in business. Women are strongly advised to read such books as Betty Harragan's *Games Your Mother Never Taught You* and *The Managerial Woman*. Here we will try to add a few observations that have been either overlooked or minimized by previous writers.

Make no mistake, women will play an increasingly important role in business at all levels. The forces underlying this development are powerful and pervasive. First, the women's movement obviously has awakened an interest in many women to pursue careers. This force alone is significant but it is magnified by even more powerful economic forces. More women will have to work to maintain the standard of living they want. Inflation combined with the instability of family relationships is forcing most women to prepare for a career that can support them. Finally, discrimination against women in business is diminishing, not only because of the law, but because employers are finding women can do the jobs just as well, if not better, as the men they have been hiring.

WHAT WE HAVE LEARNED

So far what we have learned about women in business has largely destroyed the myths and folklore that have barred them from many jobs. Two decades ago you would have been a candidate for the loony bin if you even suggested that women could be police officers, fire fighters, truck drivers, automobile mechanics, or industrial sales representatives. We have learned that women can do most things previously thought to be the sole domain of men.

Second, we have learned that many of the problems management foresaw if they hired women for some jobs have just not materialized. Perhaps the author's study in the field of industrial selling is a case in point. In 1978, forty-six industrial saleswomen working the Dallas metropolitan area were personally interviewed concerning their jobs and the problems they faced in breaking into industrial selling. In parallel with the study of the saleswomen, their sales managers were also interviewed. In every case the problems expected to be disclosed by the saleswomen and their sales managers failed to materialize, as related in the following items.

Item: Women will have trouble handling the entertainment side of selling. Not so. The saleswomen in the study all said that they had no problems with entertainment. Most of them said that they simply didn't do any and that their customers didn't seem to want to be entertained. When entertainment was called for, the saleswoman and her spouse would take out the buyer and his spouse for a foursome on the town. Clearly, entertainment simply was not the problem it was perceived to be earlier.

Item: The newly hired industrial saleswoman would encounter a great deal of trouble with the existing salesmen. Not so. The women said that they found their fellow salespeople to be supportive very quickly.

Item: The saleswoman's family would prove to be a problem. Not so. It was reported that the husbands were very supportive of their wives' jobs and that their family lives were even more harmonious than before. Perhaps the additional money coming into the household would help explain this phenomenon.

Item: Male buyers wouldn't accept industrial saleswomen technically. Not so. There was not one instance in which a saleswoman reported difficulty in making a sale because the buyer did not respect her technical expertise. A bit of thought on this matter will disclose the logic of this finding. First, all salespeople must establish their technical expertise. Second, there are some simple techniques that communicate one's expertise to the buyer early in the sale. Finally, experienced professional buyers know that no first-rate company ever allows a sales rep—either man or woman—without technical training needed to do the job to make a call.

Item: Women can't sell industrial goods. Not so. Each of the forty-six industrial saleswomen interviewed was successfully selling industrial products and their success was confirmed by their sales managers. By and large, the most significant finding of the research showed little difference between the industrial saleswoman and the industrial salesman. The biggest problem the saleswomen voiced was overcoming their lack of self-confidence. This topic will be examined in detail shortly.

The more we study this matter of women in business, the more evidence we accumulate that most of the hypothesized differences between men and women in business careers are largely conjecture. In an article in the September 1979 issue of the *Academy of Management Journal*, (p. 539), in which career planning was studied, no differences were found to exist between men and women in the matter of their career planning activities. Our study of industrial saleswomen similarly showed that the hypotheses originally developed concerning the problems women would encounter in industrial sales simply weren't supported by the evidence collected in the field.

Self-Confidence

Previously mentioned was that women have reported the biggest problem they encountered upon entering business was their lack of self-confidence. It's not that women genetically lack self-confidence: anyone in their position and with their background experience would lack self-confidence. Anyone lacks self-confidence who hasn't had the experiences to gain it. A frequent question asked is, "If self-confidence is so important, then how do I get it?" The answer is that you can only get it through experience, by doing things and learning that you can do them. The athlete initially lacks self-confidence. Rookies are unsure of themselves for they don't know what they can do and a bit of experience will clearly tell them. The best advice is simply not to worry about self-confidence. You will gain it as time passes and nothing drastic will happen if you fail. People worry about their self-confidence because they are afraid of failing. Once you get rid of the fear of failing, then the problem of self-confidence resolves itself.

In ridding yourself of the fear of failing, it helps if you come to realize that the world isn't going to end and that really nothing very serious is going to happen to you if you fail in some endeavor. Suppose you do fail in your job and get fired. So what? There are plenty of other jobs. You're not going to starve to death. People aren't going to walk down the street pointing their fingers at you while laughing. Failure is not nearly the ogre that we make it to be. Almost every successful person has failed many times in one way or another, but they learn to live with their failures and learn from them. It is through these experiences in dealing with failure that you will develop self-confidence.

Games Some Women Play

Beverly Miles, owner of Parkhurst Publications, and co-author with me of a book on industrial saleswomen, has identified five self-destructive games she has observed women playing. They are:

1. Soap opera
2. Poor little me
3. Take care of me
4. Cute little girl
5. Seduction

Soap Opera Beverly talks at great length about how many women live soap opera lives and try to bring them into the office. That's a no-no in business: your personal life should be left at home. The boss really isn't interested in hearing about the trials and tribulations of your marriage or love affairs or all of the juicy neighborhood scandals. Some people live such soap opera lives and scheme to enmesh their coworkers in their problems.

One woman who was manager of a small distributive organization had been living a most traumatic existence. Three years previously she and her former husband had gone through bankruptcy. Since that time the sheriff had been routinely knocking at her door for a bad check or her children's misdeeds. Every week she had a new boyfriend, would you know, who was going to marry her. Each day the tales she spun beat anything that has ever been on a television soap opera. The boss was fascinated by the stories only because he simply couldn't believe what he heard. He also noticed that the general manager's personal problems were severely affecting the business. Then she "unofficially" borrowed some money to cover some bad checks. More and more of her time was taken just handling her personal life. Finally, the relationship had to end, and both parties lost because she did have some needed virtues. She was a hard worker with initiative who was willing to run the entire operation alone at times when the owner had to be out of town selling, which was quite often. Even though it was most difficult to replace her, living her soap opera life destroyed her job. Be most discreet about involving your work group with your personal problems. And Beverly Miles says that some men are guilty of playing the same game.

Poor Little Me Some people, in an attempt to gain sympathy from their superiors, love to tell tales of how the world so grossly mistreated them. They can talk for hours about their misfortunes and complain that the world has continually given them the short end of the deal. Poor little me! This game is a blatant attempt to gain favorable treatment from the boss so he or she will be somewhat reluctant to fire or otherwise impose managerial dictates upon the employee. Obviously, this is not a healthy business relationship. Even the individual's colleagues resent attempts to gain favor through these whining tales.

Take Care of Me Many women who come into the business world try to assume the same relationship they have with their husbands: "Take care of me." They expect their fellow workers to help them out, to do their work, to protect them, and to hold their hand. Well, it doesn't work that way in business. Fellow workers resent being expected to nursemaid a colleague. After all, they have careers of their own to worry about and have their own jobs to do. One of the biggest complaints that policemen and firemen have about the introduction of women into those careers is that they're afraid that they'd have to spend too much time taking care of the women in difficult situations. When push comes to shove, they have all they can do to take care of themselves. Thus the slightest evidence that the individual expects to be taken care of will not be greeted with favor. Indeed, it is very important that the woman make it clear that she can take care of herself and is not looking for undue support from her colleagues.

Cute Little Girl Some women come into a business organization and try to gain favor by playing the cute little girl game. They're always dressed most femininely and adopt behavior mannerisms that work wonders when dealing with men in social situations. They clearly expect to advance in business the same way they have advanced themselves socially throughout their lives. This behavior seldom works and most assuredly will engender **a great deal of antagonism throughout the organization because the people who are really doing the work will resent efforts to compete on any basis other than productivity.**

Seduction Little needs to be said about sexuality in business for it is one of the most popular topics written about in books on women in business. There have been cases in which women have used sex as a basis for advancing their careers. They feel that they can sleep their way to the top. While most of the writers take a Victorian stance that such tactics never work, I cannot help but wonder if they have been paying attention. Now don't get this next statement wrong for an instant, for I do not approve of this tactic or game and I will say that it can lead to a great deal of difficulty. But I have personally observed situations where certain women did advance themselves beyond their business capabilities through the adroit seduction of their superiors. Now make no mistake about it, such behavior infuriates the rest of the organization and in each of the cases that I have observed the superior and the woman were destroyed in the organization by the seduction. Most astute business executives know it's a bad mistake to mix sex and business and will move quickly to remove anyone from the organization who is confusing the purpose of their job. Thus in the short run seduction may seem a profitable game to play, but to my observation it will likely lead to trouble. Now, in all honesty, several of the women using the game eventually married the executive with whom they were playing the game but they did so while working elsewhere. And I often wonder how comfortable a life they can lead knowing their husband's behavior toward willing female subordinates.

It is important to realize that you don't have to use seduction as a competitive tool and that those who do are apt to quickly encounter grave difficulties in the organization.

Summary

This section can be summarized with six bits of advice. First, all of the previous advice on career management for men applies equally to the careers of women in business. Few adjustments are needed for the business careers of men and women simply aren't that much different. Second, in the future women are going to be pursuing business careers in greater and greater numbers. Women are a fact of business life. The women's movement is not a passing fancy but has its feet solidly based in the economics of the times. Women are going to have business careers because economically they must. Third, right now men are afraid of women in business because they don't know what to expect of them. They're uncertain of how to relate to women on a business level, because they have enough trouble trying to find ways of relating to them socially. They look at women as time bombs that can go off any minute. Thus, the astute woman goes out of her way to allay these fears among her male coworkers. She finds ways of alleviating their perceived risks about her. Experience finds that these worries can be easily dispensed with and are not a major problem. Fourth, the women must understand that business is a game and that politics is the key to advancement in most organizations. She must learn that just putting in long, hard hours and being loyal is not enough. It's a game, and if you don't know how to play it you'll be a loser. Fifth, it takes a certain amount of toughness to survive because the basic nature of business is competitive, thus the good jobs that the woman wants will also be coveted by others. Thus if one is unwilling to advance herself at the expense of others, she'll not go far. It takes a certain amount of toughness to meet the failures in business, to accept the criticism of superiors, to hang in there day after day doing a job that isn't always very pleasant. It takes some toughness to come to work in the morning when you're not feeling well. Finally, don't worry about the locker room syndrome. The woman does not have to become one of the boys in order to succeed in business. The men are going to get together in their poker games, golf outings, or whatever. But that doesn't mean that it will be wise for the women to try to crack into that group.

PART 6

Increasing
Your
Productivity

Productivity: The Key to Your Success

One hears the word productivity bandied about in intellectual circles these days. Economists blame much of our inflation and many of our economic problems on our seeming inability to increase our national productivity sufficiently. In agonizing over our national productivity, it is only natural that some attention would be focused on the productivity of the individual. Many articles in trade journals mention the need for managing your time more wisely, thus increasing your productivity. Several books have been written on the proper management of time, and time management has become a popular topic for management seminars and discussions in executive suites. This phenomenon is both good and bad: good because we are recognizing the importance of productivity in our affairs; bad because the term has become somewhat of a cliche, thus it tends to be relegated to the conceptual trash bin. Productivity is far too important to our lives to be treated lightly. You are strongly urged to consider your work habits most carefully to discover ways that you can become more effective—more productive. But before we go further, let us define what we are talking about.

What is Productivity?

Although many people try to make the concept as complex as possible, it is really extremely simple: productivity is how much value one creates from some fixed unit of work; it is a ratio of output to input. A highly productive person or organization gets more output per manhour of effort than a relatively unproductive person or organization. Productivity is closely related to the concept of efficiency, which, in a machine, is the ratio of output to input. Unfortunately, the term efficiency has gained such a bad reputation in some circles that we tend to disdain its usage.

Naturally, from the viewpoint of the total economic system we are greatly interested in productivity, for it essentially determines the goods and services we can produce (our output) from the resources we devote to the effort (our input). Limited resources make it even more important to get as much output as possible from them.

You are interested in your productivity, for, in the end, it determines the size of your paycheck. Nowhere is that more evident than in the field of selling where one's earnings may be directly tied to productivity through the compensation plan. The more sold—the more output—the more earnings. However, the high-earning sales rep may not be the most productive, for he may have obtained his productivity by spending an unusually large number of hours working. His earnings per hour worked may not be as high as those of some more talented individual who is able to earn a lot more from his time. Essentially, we all sell our time. We only have so many hours in a day to work; the person able to do the most with those hours (has talent?) seems to fare best. And so this section dwells on how to get more output from the time you spend working. Naturally, the more time you work, given an efficiency rate, the more your total output will be. One of the reasons many people seek a high rate of productivity is that it allows them to work fewer hours thus having more leisure.

What This Section Hopes to Do for You

First, we will try to stress the importance of productivity to you personally, how it affects your career and earnings. Second, we will try to convince you that you can increase your productivity if you want to do so, that your output is not something preordained and programmed into your system by the powers above. You can increase your productivity by taking several definite steps. All that is needed is your desire to do so. Third, we will discuss various techniques you can use for increasing your output.

This section was prompted by my relationship with Warren G. who had been a colleague of mine for several years and had, at various social functions, managed to drag me into a corner for a conversation which he always started off by saying, "I really want to know your secret for doing all the work you do. How do you do it?" Not being too interested in spending the next few hours telling him, particularly at a cocktail party, I always shrugged my shoulders and evaded the whole scene by mumbling some generality such as "Put in a lot of hours, I guess," or "I think it's called hard work," and then sought out more charming people to talk to.

However, Warren was persistent; he simply wouldn't drop the question. Somehow he finally realized that I was not going to talk about it at parties so he changed tactics. He tried a straightforward approach by coming into the office one day, sitting down, and asking a much better thought-out series of questions concerning my work habits. He confided that he was extremely unhappy with his output. "I just don't seem to be able to get anything out. I haven't written anything in a year despite my sternest intentions. I am bogged down and need help badly if I'm going to stay in teaching." I knew this to be true for Warren had been passed over once for tenure because his output was unsatisfactory to both his peers and the administration. Warren needed help. With that direct approach, I could no longer avoid verbalizing my philosophies on being productive. Most of this material simply formalizes what I told Warren in our next several hours of conversation.

The next year Warren wrote four articles and began a book, which was subsequently finished the following year. He has had no difficulty with his productivity since that time. He could do the work; it was just that he had not figured out how. Much of his progress had been blocked by several myths about work commonly believed to be true. Three of the myths that Warren first attacked are the subjects of the next section.

Some Myths

Before we delve into the positive side of increasing your productivity, let us clear away some cobwebs—myths—that continually seem to get in our way.

Myth No. 1: Productivity is largely a matter of keeping one's nose to the grindstone—working hard and long.

Some people have accomplished their goals by working long, hard hours, but as we have indicated before, this is not productivity. These people pay a frightful price for their output. Not only does their input include long hours, but it also may have a detrimental influence on health, relationships with family, and personal happiness—a frightful input.

Interestingly, the highly productive people in the world spend relatively few hours accomplishing their tasks. They turn out a great deal of value and have remaining time to enjoy life, which after all, is what we are ultimately after. We've all known many people who spend an ungodly amount of time in the office. The hours they work are staggering, yet there is little visible output.

Leonard worked for me at one school, and I don't think I have ever known a more diligent teacher. He was in his office all day long preparing for his classes and seeing students. He was there many times when no one else was around; I was told that he frequently came in at night and on weekends. Yet we fired Leonard because he had not produced anything. Not only had be failed to write a single word, but his student ratings were totally unsatisfactory—his productivity in the classroom did not exist. Hours are not the sole answer; he was a terrible teacher. Now don't jump to the erroneous conclusion that productive people don't have to work some hours. Normally you have to put in some hours working if you want to accomplish your tasks. It is just that hours alone won't do it: the hours must be productive.

Dan was a hard-working electrical engineer who spent long hours in the lab seven days a week. He loved the work so it was no big sacrifice, particularly since he was still single, but he had little to show for his time. Finally, his superior had to give him a poor quarterly evaluation for lack of results, which brought Dan into the office for some talk about productivity. The first hurdle obviously blocking our conversation was Dan's insistence that he was productive because he spent so much time in the lab. He revolted when shocked by the statement, "We don't really care how many hours you work. All that counts is what you produce that we can use." Dan still clings to the hours theory and also just barely clings to his job.

We are still hung up culturally with the idea that hours are equivalent to productivity. We find managers requiring people to stay in their offices from 8:00 A.M.

until the last dog is dead in the evening. They chain employees to desks and expect them to stay there. But there are exceptions.

Laura was president of a small, profitable advertising agency. She told her people, "I don't care if I ever see you in the place. I don't care what time you get to work or what time you leave. All I care about is that you do the jobs I assign you." Thereupon Laura would lay a great deal of work on each individual. She forced their productivity and was sensible enough to know that she would not get it merely by chaining them to their desks. She realized that many times the company got more productivity out of an individual if he was able to work at home the whole day. Little is accomplished in some offices during regular business hours because the office is too chaotic. Thus, never make the mistake of thinking that by putting in hours at the office you are being productive. The two may have little to do with one another. You may sit behind a desk for 100 hours and produce nothing of value. You must find ways of spending those hours in a productive environment.

Myth No. 2: Doing something is being productive.

A person may fall in the water and splash a great deal of water yet drown. Just splashing water around does not mean one is swimming. A halfback can run from sideline to sideline until he is out of breath and lose yardage. Similarly, a person can do a great many things and still be nonproductive. Some writers believe that they must sit down in front of a typewriter each day and put some ink on the paper, regardless of its content. I met Helen one evening at a writer's round-table meeting in Hollywood where the subject was productivity. She was holding forth her philosophies. Every morning she sat down in front of the typewriter at 9:00 A.M. with the coffee pot

---

and stayed there until noon, putting words on paper regardless of what they were. She used a great deal of paper, but after five years she had yet to sell anything. The group looked over her output; she was just splashing water. She had nothing to say and would not know how to say it if she did. She had created nothing of value to her or anyone else, despite all of her efforts and motion.

Productivity is not effort and it is not motion. It is not a matter of doing things. It is a matter of doing things that have value to you—creating value. If something has no value to you, then you were not productive when you created it. Moreover, most likely that activity was counterproductive in that it prevented you from doing something of value.

Myth No. 3: Good organization is the earmark of the productive person.

Leonard, the terrible teacher we had to fire, was the most organized person I have seen in teaching. He developed detailed course outlines supported by meticulous notes. Each day was planned the night before just like all the productivity experts urge. But there was little output valued by anyone. Organization does not guarantee valuable output. Indeed, some people become so intent on organization that they spend far too much effort achieving it and too little getting out the work. Should you still cling to this myth, just remember that the bureaucratic red tape everyone screams about is merely the tangible evidence of a highly organized effort.

Ways to Increase Your Output

So far we have been negative in telling you what doesn't automatically increase your productivity. Now let's examine some techniques for increasing your output that perhaps you have not considered. No one of these or even all of them put together assures a high output from you, but they will help if you apply them with some intelligence and good judgment which are the real keys to creating value.

TOOL UP FOR THE JOB

Of all the keys to productivity, preparation has perplexed me more than any of the others, because its truth seems so self-evident, yet it is so widely ignored, at least by the people with whom I have had contact. If you intended to manufacture men's shirts, you would obtain a plant and fill it with the right machines. You would tool up for the job. It is well established in production management that if one is to get high productivity one must be properly tooled up, which today means buying automatic equipment and a modern plant. Production managers are well aware of all of the principles of increasing the productivity of a manufacturing plant. Well, what are you but a manufacturing plant? The principles of producing an automobile are no different than the principles for increasing your personal productivity. Here I must again dwell upon my personal experiences, for this was one of the first principles of personal productivity I stumbled across.

I remember well my freshman year at Indiana when we were taking accounting. Oh, how all the frat brothers used to complain about that accounting course—the long hours slaving over working papers, trying to find the two cents to balance an account. None of them had adding machines, and it was rather obvious that most of their time was spent simply adding figures, making mistakes, then trying to find those mistakes. I bought an old

Remington-Rand printing calculator. I needed the printing calculator, for I foresaw the same problem in a coming statistics course in which there would be need for multiplication and division. Suddenly accounting became very easy. I would do the accounting assignments in a small fraction of the time that those blockheads were spending chasing down their errors. Thereupon I proceeded to buy an electric typewriter, which in those days was quite a rarity. IBM had not made inroads in the used market so an old Underwood, one of their first electric models, was my prize possession. Again my productivity leaped over that of my competitors who were burdened by either having to write out their reports longhand and suffer the wrath of the professors who could not read their scrawls, or having to punch out papers on the old manual typewriters. The money invested in those two machines paid dividends beyond imagination. I could not even begin to count the rewards reaped from them.

Since that time I have firmly believed in tooling up for the job. I am willing to invest in whatever equipment appears useful for increasing my productivity. These very words are being spoken into a dictating machine during a drive across the desert between Las Vegas and Los Angeles, a productivity-increasing activity that will be discussed later.

One principle of production management holds that one should not keep using a machine just because it works. If something more productive comes along, it should replace the inferior equipment. I am now dictating on a little, portable Panasonic that I purchased because my old, larger machine was relatively inefficient and at times lost part of what I was saying. It was counterproductive. I bought an IBM Selectric when it first came out and it still works fine but I had to buy the Selectric II with the error correcting feature because that innovation greatly increases my output. In my car I have a built-in tape recorder for dictation. More will be said of this later. At this time I am in the process of buying a home computer and word-processing system on which to write and store these words. The list does not stop there, but I will not bore you further with the equipment that I collect. It is all for one purpose: to help me create more value in a shorter amount of time.

Almost inevitably, when I lay this philosophy on anyone, I hear the protest, "But all that costs money! You may have the money, but I don't!" Well, when I was in college I did not have the money either. There is always money for the things you want to do. The student who protests that he does not have money for such things and then spends his dollars drinking beer at the local pub and driving a Corvette fails to impress me with his protests. I counter by saying, "When you buy equipment to do a better job, you are investing in yourself and in your future. If you know a better place to put your money, you're in trouble!"

It is staggering to hear the pitiful excuses of people who resist the idea of tooling up to do a better job. People are earning good salaries who spend money for this gimcrack and that one, who put thousands of dollars in the stock market investing in other people's concerns, and yet who are unwilling to invest relatively few dollars in themselves. It seems patently ridiculous to me why anyone would be willing to hand money over to someone else to invest in some enterprise, yet be unwilling to invest in his own enterprises. The only conclusion is that the person has more faith in the other party than in himself, and if that is the case then there is scant hope for that individual. A person of merit should be willing to invest money in himself. I know of no better investment that will pay such large dividends. When you invest in yourself you have control of that investment. You are not dependent upon the abilities of other people and you are continually paid dividends.

An interesting sidelight to this matter of having the proper equipment is that when you have such equipment you tend to be willing to do burdensome jobs that you otherwise try to avoid doing. Naturally, the particular pieces of equipment that will help you to be more productive depend upon the nature of your calling. An artist would probably want a full studio. An engineer might want a fairly large programmable computer. A business executive might want a fully-equipped home office with electric typewriter, desk-top calculator, copy machine, dictating machine, or home computer. A large desk and work table are most helpful; and file cabinets are needed for your information if any semblance of efficiency is to be achieved.

LEVERAGE YOUR TIME

The concept of leverage has been well established in the financial world. It means financing your business with other people's money—leverage your own limited funds by using them as a basis for borrowing other people's money. You can leverage your productivity by learning to borrow or use other people's time. Doing something yourself that someone else can do for you makes little sense, even though it may take them longer to do it.

Here the excellent secretary comes into the picture. Many executives know that they owe a great deal of their success to their secretaries. A good secretary takes all of the burdensome details off your hands and lets you spend your time doing the things that must have your attention. Your secretary blocks off the rest of the world so as not to waste your time needlessly. After I have finished dictating these words, the cassette will be transcribed by Marsha Kolar. Now I could sit down and type these same words, but she does a far better job of it much more quickly, thus leaving me to my main task of creating the words, getting the thoughts out into the open. From that point onward I try to let others do the work for me because they can really do the work better than I can. But more importantly, it frees me for creating things of value. This is how I leverage my time. I also have a secretary at SMU who takes care of all of the detail work connected with the academic part of my job.

Why universities do not provide their faculty with more assistance has always been unfathomable to me. Deans and department heads spend endless hours complaining about how unproductive their faculty members are, and yet they seem to go out of their way to make it as difficult as possible for these people to be productive. They provide inadequate offices, scant secretarial help, practically no equipment, and usually an inadequate amount of research assistance. It would seem that if an administrator truly wanted to increase the faculty's productivity, the least he could do would be to see that they were properly equipped and staffed with people. Yet you see professors earning $25,000 a year running errands around the campus that a $4-an-hour part-time office helper could do. A good assistant is certainly one key to increasing your productivity. If your boss will not give you an assistant, you might consider paying for one out of your own pocket.

Look at the lessons modern physicians have learned about increasing their productivity, causing complaints from most of their patients. Nevertheless, they are creating more value per hour than previously. First, each doctor has several examination rooms so that patients can get prepared for his attention. The doctor does not have to stand around waiting, wasting time, while a patient gets undressed or has his temperature or blood pressure taken. Nurses take care of all the formalities, such as taking temperature, blood pressure, weight, and filling out papers. The doctor tries to spend his or her time making diagnoses and recommending treatments, even delegating much of the remedial action—giving shots or medicine—to the nurses. The doctor moves from room to room listening to the stories, thumping here and there, and making diagnoses or recommending action, all very efficient and most productive, even though violating some other principles of human relations. People who are there to have their hands held don't like it, and there is a good bit of insecurity in all of us. However, here we are only talking about productivity.

Lawyers now have legal aides to help them with the details of their profession. Supreme court justices could not function without the law clerks doing their research. Their work load is backbreaking; they must leverage their time. Presidents of large corporations have long recognized these needs and have created the staff position, assistant to the president, in order to delegate certain tasks to other people.

The concept of getting other people to do work for you, while very simple, is still an extremely important way to increase your productivity. You must find ways of bestowing upon others the honor of doing your work. Or to put it more kindly, do not try to do everything yourself. Realize that many people can help you if you will but let them in on your act.

USE YOUR DOWN-TIME OR WASTED TIME

As mentioned previously, these words were dictated during a drive across the Mohave Desert. This five-hour drive to Los Angeles would be a total waste of time, but through the good graces of a dictating machine I hope that I am able to salvage these otherwise wasted hours.

We all waste a great deal of time—sometimes deliberately, more often we are forced to waste time. We spend an hour on the freeway getting to work—a waste of time. We sit twiddling our thumbs in an office waiting to see a customer—a waste of time. You are on a four-hour flight to New York—a waste of time. Situations arise almost daily in which we can do nothing simply because of the circumstances of waiting for someone else or traveling. People living in large metropolitan centers such as Los Angeles waste a lot of time driving around. Many people have found ways to put this time to good use. One key to using otherwise wasted time is to be continually prepared to make use of that time. If you are going on a trip, then think about the work you can do while traveling and prepare to do it. If you are a sales rep waiting in a purchasing agent's waiting room, you might have some paperwork handy. Perhaps you could write some letters. Correspondence always needs to be done.

You may be able to take this book or some other material along to catch up on your reading, thus freeing yourself for other work at times normally reserved for reading. After all, any professional person worth his salt must keep up with his field and this requires a great deal of reading, not only of journals and periodicals, but also of books. Rare is the individual who has time to do all the reading. Almost universally we complain that we cannot keep up with our fields. The key is learning how to do this reading in otherwise wasted time.

Perhaps nowhere is wasted time so evident than when watching television. Although the Madison Avenue crowd no doubt will wince at reading this, perhaps few things are such a big waste of time as the commercial breaks. The amount of reading you can do during the commercials on television is amazing if you simply have one of your journals or books handy at all times.

DON'T LET PEOPLE WASTE YOUR TIME

John was a particularly likeable, able young man, but he had yet to produce anything despite his promise. The years rolled by and still John had not produced. Eight years after he had completed his course work for his doctorate he still had to complete his dissertation. Each summer he would return to his alma mater with good intentions of finishing it up but it just did not happen. The reason became rather obvious when I investigated the situation, as I was asked to do by the tenure committee. John was a nice guy and that was his trouble. He liked to talk and people liked to talk to him, and therein was the root to John's unproductive life: he let everyone waste his time. He complained about not getting anything done because people continually streamed into his office; I sat there and watched the parade. He encouraged it: he let anyone waste an hour talking about absolutely nothing of relevance—just shooting the breeze. John wasted time and let other people waste time for him. He was an extreme case and you might say, "Well, other people were not wasting his time. He was wasting it himself." That is true.

Perhaps Harry would be a more appropriate example. Harry had good intentions and did not encourage people to waste his time, but the net result was the same. Harry could not say no, so people would ask him to lunch with a group of visiting firemen from who-knows-where. To be accommodating, Harry would allow himself to be talked into going and then complain for days afterward about the three hours he lost talking to people about nothing of importance.

Some people find it necessary to become absolutely vicious to the point of being outright rude in order to stop others from wasting their time. Colleagues just get in the habit of stopping by to pass the time and manage to pass the day. Perhaps a locked door will convey the message. Sometimes you simply have to excuse yourself. Sometimes in order to avoid such situations executives have a hidden office to which they can flee in order to get some work done. One sales manager, when getting behind on paperwork, manages to "take a trip into the field to supervise some sales rep." He goes home and spends three or four days getting caught up. He knows that if he goes to the office he will be a dead duck for everyone there will conspire to waste his time and he will not get the work done.

Clever people have learned to arrange many subterfuges in order to get productive time alone. One highly placed civil servant finally got fed up with the situation and placed this sign over her desk: "If what you have to tell me isn't important, then why are you here?" Well, one could pay a rather dear price for such rudeness, but the point is that some people are forced to go to extremes to keep the loafers out.

I remember in particular one individual who would regularly drop in and chat for about an hour every day.

He was politicking, out passing on the gossip, and trying to find new gossip. That was all he wanted. He wasted an enormous amount of my time.

Do not jump to the conclusion that a little bit of exchange is not needed, for it certainly is. One cannot divorce oneself from the work group. You must have some social interchange but this is a matter of balance: how much time is spent and at what point does it get in the way of your work? There is a place for dropping by people's offices to socialize.

PERFECTION CAN BE COSTLY

Ernie was a perfectionist who wrote his papers in school over and over until every word was perfect. Naturally, Ernie exerted about four times the effort of others who got A minuses on their papers, yet in the end they all got A's in the course—identical payoff. Granted, some purists might insist that Ernie learned far more with his diligence than did his less dutiful peers, but it is doubtful that he learned four times as much. Interestingly, after graduation Ernie wrote nothing. His standards of perfection were such that he was unable to create anything that satisfied him; thus his standards prevented him from doing anything. If you seek perfection in everything you do, you will do very little.

Many productive people are more oriented toward getting the job done in a workable or satisfactory way than they are in producing a perfect product. In most cases perfection takes far more time than its rewards are worth. During the early 1950s many of our military people were prone to put down the Russian military equipment as shoddy. They would point to Soviet tanks as evidencing extremely crude workmanship and brag about the superior fineries of our own equipment—our welding seams were ground down smooth. Big deal! We have not heard much of that nonsense since the Korean War. The Soviet hardware, crude though it may have been, did the job as well as our own. We paid a dear price for some of our perfection.

Our zero-defects programs are exceedingly costly and hinder productivity. Many times the total productivity of an organization can be enhanced if one is willing to accept a slightly lesser quality. Learn to live with some defects. Remember that many things we consider defective are nevertheless completely functional. Take the matter of a golf ball. Golfers are willing to pay $1.35 for first-line golf balls. Golf balls not meeting quality standards are sold as "X-outs": the brand name has been X-ed out. These balls sell for a much lower price of 75 cents. Most golfers find the defective ball to be every bit as functional as the first-line item. Discount stores frequently sell seconds or imperfects for a lower price that are difficult to distinguish from the first-line article. Tires with blemishes are less expensive, yet deliver the same results. Perfection costs money.

Now do not rush out and use these words as a license to do shoddy work. That will get you nowhere. Certainly you must produce work up to the standards needed for the job. The message here is simply that you should not spend an unduly large amount of time trying to write the perfect letter or the perfect report. Rather, try to create one that does the job and let it go at that.

Admittedly, in some professions we do want to aim at perfection. You would not care to have a surgeon operate on you who was willing to go for a 70 percent satisfaction rate. And you would not care to fly in an airplane put together with slipshod work. Still, in each of those instances the people involved are not perfect, but then who is perfect? The point is that they strive for the perfection that is required in those fields. Only you can determine the extent to which perfection is needed in your career.

AVOID MEETINGS LIKE THE PLAGUE

Somewhere in the nether regions of Hell there resides a sadistic soul to whom Satan has delegated the job of stifling productivity. He was awarded the devil's highest honors for creating the committee meeting. More time than we can possibly calculate is wasted, irretrievably lost, sitting in pointless meetings, listening to banalities, rediscovering the wheel, and tolerating the stupidity of one's peers while trying to lead them onto the path of truth and righteousness.

Highly productive people abhor meetings, particularly committee meetings. Productive people cannot tolerate being unproductive for it offends the very marrow of their bones; they will not allow others to diminish their productivity. Indeed, they may become downright mean in their insistence on being allowed to be productive. Long ago perceptive faculty members learned that faculty meetings were largely a waste of time—attended mostly by those who want to play campus lawyer. Many schools have a difficult time raising a quorum at such meetings and their deans wonder why. The answer is simple: the meetings are a waste of time where nothing is done. The perceptive faculty member recognizes such meetings and avoids them.

Business is not so fortunate, for employees are not given a choice of attending meetings called by their superiors. The meeting is a command performance and to be absent jeopardizes one's position. Thus it is incumbent upon the perceptive manager to fight tenaciously his tendency to call meetings if he sincerely wants to increase the productivity of his work group. Meetings should have a very definite reason and should be conducted in a disciplined manner in which problems are attacked. People who want to burden their colleagues with oratory need to be controlled by the group leader. Finally, definite time limits should be set on meetings and the leader should fight to keep on schedule.

There is much you can do to minimize the time you waste in meetings. First, avoid joining groups that meet unless you have a definite interest in their work. Do not be a joiner just to have something to put on your resume. You must learn to say no when you really feel like it. Do not feel compelled to volunteer because of social pressures. When someone suggests a meeting, be willing to ask if the meeting is really needed. Many times the same ends can be achieved by telephone calls with no real need to bring people together in a face-to-face confrontation. Many individuals call meetings to save time at your expense; he does not care if he wastes your time. Do not play that game. If you have a given contribution to make that will not be affected by other people's opinions, then you may give your opinions or thoughts to the leader and let him use them for what they may be worth. You have no real need to attend the meeting.

Meetings are valuable when you need an exchange of ideas from people for arriving at a plan of action or making a decision. Again, do not jump to the conclusion that meetings are not necessary; some of them are. What I am saying is that a large percentage of them are not and an even larger percentage are so inefficiently run that they waste a great deal of time.

LEARN TO SAY NO

The previous section intimated that there are times you should say no. Remember the plight of John who could not complete his doctoral dissertation because he could not say no to people.

Admittedly, saying no is a difficult thing to learn in this day and age when we are preaching the development of interpersonal relationships. Somehow we believe that we must say yes to make people like us, that if we say no we are rejecting them and somehow this will make us unpopular. Popularity all depends upon how well you learn how to say no. Some people have learned the art extremely well. Naturally they do not coldly reject things; they have nice ways of indicating that they cannot take on an obligation. You must learn to focus your time on the important things and weed out the useless. Yet we all get saddled doing things we really do not want to do. We sit through boring luncheons wondering why on earth we are there, wishing we were somewhere else. We are at a convention in Timbuktu wondering how we got there. Well, it was because we have not learned how to say no or we have not realistically evaluated the conditions of the commitment we made.

Roger was clever at saying no. The dialogue would go something like this: "Gee, I'd really enjoy doing something like that, but I've just taken on this contract that must be completed by the end of the month and I'm sorry, but I just couldn't do justice to your group." Many times Roger would beg off unwanted luncheons or dinners by simply claiming a previous engagement.

What is the point of going to lunch with someone, wasting two or three hours while getting fatter, when you are not accomplishing something you want to do? This is particularly true in situations when you have a certain amount of prestige that others want to use to enhance their own projects. They feel that your presence adds luster to their relationships with their luncheon companions. Thus, you find your colleagues inviting you out to lunch with a certain person and you sit there wondering why. You must learn not to let yourself be used, for these people are wasting your time.

LEARN TO BLOCK OFF YOUR CALENDAR

Your secretary can sometimes get you into unwanted situations unknowingly. You intend to spend all day Friday playing golf or working on something or other. Your secretary books you for a luncheon or meeting with some visiting firemen and the day is shot. If you want to block off a day, then the minute you make that decision tell your secretary to make no appointments that day under any circumstances. If your situation is not that final, at least make certain that your secretary clears any appointments with you on that day. Again, it may pay you to "leave town." Learn to get lost.

LEARN TO USE THE TELEPHONE

Alexander Graham Bell gave us one of the greatest time savers or time wasters imaginable. Which it is is up to you. Admittedly, some people hang on the horn for hours, just passing the time, but this is obvious and certainly easily correctable if one desires. So let us focus upon the time-saving aspects of the telephone.

Many large businesses have come to realize the efficiency of telephoning people rather than communicating by letter. The letter is not an efficient communications medium. First, while many penny-pinching executives scream about the cost of a phone call, saying you can send a letter for 15 cents, they are totally mistaken. A letter does not cost 15 cents; it is much more expensive, many times in excess of the cost of a telephone call, particularly if the call is on a WATS line. Time is needed to write a letter, then your secretary has to transcribe it. Usually certain things are left unsaid, so the receiver must respond and you must again write additional letters. Perhaps several letters exchange hands before the matter is settled. Yet the whole issue could have been settled with one phone call to exchange ideas. It may take you half an hour to write a letter when a five-minute phone call could settle the whole affair. Again, this is a matter of learning how to leverage your time. Let Ma Bell work instead of you. Okay, so your telephone bills are going to run into three figures! So what! Keep your mind on the end value created and you usually will find the results to be worth the investments. Naturally, if you can get someone else to do your telephoning for you, so much the better. Your secretary or assistant can make many of your phone calls. When you are simply looking for information, let others run it down: learn to use other legs.

BE READY TO WORK

Remember Helen who would sit at her typewriter three hours each morning trying to force some output that simply wouldn't come? One of her problems was that she was not ready to work; she was fighting it. Your productivity will be vastly enhanced if you are ready to work when you begin. Be eager to work, want to tear into it and get it done. And eagerness is difficult to force. If you fundamentally want to be out doing something else, your productivity will not be impressive. Again, I will resort to my own experiences.

I cannot recall ever failing to do something I wanted to do while in college because I had to study. Studying was always the last thing on the agenda. If there was a good show in town or my friends wanted to go to the local pub or we had some other action such as a game to play, I was not about to be sitting in my room studying, knowing full well that my mind was somewhere else. Not much output results under such circumstances. I would go play and then work when ready, which for me, because I'm a "night person," was late at night. I could isolate three late hours two or three nights a week and get the needed output. The key was being ready to work, wanting to get the work out. In those three hours the fur flew. Thus, while to this point you might have concluded that I advocate being a work addict, a dull grind, nothing can be further from the truth. I actually believe that play comes first. Never let work get in the way of play. The interesting reaction is that I am always eager to go to work because I know it is not interfering with anything I really want to do.

Admittedly, this may not apply in your profession. You may not have the freedoms I have to do the things I enjoy. But the principle remains that your work will be far more productive if you are eager to work when you sit down to do it. Not much is likely to happen if you are fighting it, if you want to be somewhere else, if you are not ready to work. When I sit down to write or dictate I know what I want to say, have it well in mind and organized and ready to go to it. I do not sit around trying to force it—it flows. The minute it stops flowing I quit and do something else. I do not sit around agonizing over work.

Being ready to work also means being prepared for the job, having the right equipment, supplies, and information assembled. If you are assembling a product at the end of a production line, you had best have all the parts there or you are not apt to end up with a usable product. Similarly, when you sit down to work, make certain that you have the things you need and do not have to get up continually to get a pencil, a pad of paper, or a dictionary.

Procrastination ranks high among the thieves of time. The adage, "If you want something done, give it to a busy person," has much merit. The basis for this adage is that a busy person does not have time to waste. He has to do the job and get it out of the way so he can get on to his other work. He is not going to dilly-dally over the matter. The other basis for the adage is that a busy person typically has found ways to be highly productive and thus can accommodate the new work load more easily than the inefficient person. When you are assigned a job, it will take a certain number of hours to do it. Now it does not matter whether the time is a month from now or now, it is going to take those hours. Typically what happens when you delay is that the total number of hours you spend on the task increases. I have seen a letter sit unanswered on a person's desk for a month. Daily the individual looks at the letter, thinks about it, says he must answer it, spends five or ten minutes agonizing over it, and then puts it off. The total cost of the final letter is frightful. To be most productive the correspondence should have been answered the minute it came in—just turn it right around. Highly productive people simply do not allow things to accumulate on their desks. They continually get rid of jobs.

Paula was a highly productive person in a responsible managerial position. People in her organization were continually coming into her office saying, "I have a problem. When can I see you about it?" Her answer almost inevitably, unless there was some pressing reason otherwise, would be, "Let's get it out of the way right now." She realized that the usual approach of making an appointment would take more time. Often she could handle the matter in a few moments right at that instant and get rid of it, thus increasing her own and her subordinates' productivity. If she were to tell the person to schedule a meeting through her secretary, what happens? First, the secretary's time is wasted. Next, inevitably more time is blocked out for the official meeting than is really needed, thus wasting time of both parties. Third, no one ever knows what the situation will be at the time the scheduled meeting takes place. It may interfere with some far more important matters and thus be postponed, to the detriment of everyone's productivity. Learn to get things out of the way as fast as you can. The longer they drag on, the more time it is going to take to do the job.

Life Simplification

It is rather appalling to note how complicated our lives have become. We take on so many projects and obligations that we hardly know which way to turn. Bob's plight comes to mind, although I can think of dozens of other people, including myself, whose stories would be no different. Bob was a physician, a GP. He had made good money and had invested it in various stocks, most of which were sicker than his patients. His record in the stock market (or better yet, the record of his broker in the stock market) was dismal. These matters concerned Bob a great deal, so he decided to become a venture capitalist and real estate speculator. He placed sizeable sums in various real estate syndicates and a few small businesses. His wife wanted, and got, a second home at Lake Arrowhead. Moreover, they discovered tennis and joined a tennis club when they became fairly adept at it and enjoyed participating in many of the amateur tournaments. They moved into a big, new house in a luxurious area, and the house required a great deal of time just to maintain. Bob recognized that he was on a treadmill that was rapidly increasing in speed, but he did not know what to do about it. He had committed himself to so many different activities in addition to his profession. After all, he had to go boating at Lake Arrowhead, he had to play tennis, he had to take care of managing the house, and he had to look after his investments. He saw no escape. His CPA shocked him into reality early one year: Bob was nearly bankrupt. His practice had suffered, for after all, you can only do so much business on Tuesdays and Thursdays. His work week had come down to that while his overhead went on seven days a week. His malpractice insurance had soared and the cost of the Arrowhead home combined with his residence was eating him up. Moreover, his investments were cash-eaters, not returning any cash to him, and he was having to invest more and more in the ventures. Bob was in a great deal of trouble. His life was far too complicated and those complications had hurt his productivity. He simply was not making the money he needed. Something had to give or he would be in bankruptcy. Bob could not believe it—his income was in excess of $100,000 a year and he was strapped for cash.

There were some painful scenes in the following months as Bob tightened the screws on his family. Some ultimatums were given. Some decisions had to be made, for things were going to have to go. He simplified life by getting rid of the Arrowhead property and moving into a large townhouse at Marina Del Rey where he would not be bothered with the nuisances. He stopped investing his money in enterprises that required his attention. His CPA put him in touch with one of those rare breeds, a wise investment counselor, who suggested that Bob put all of his money in municipal bonds. He would come out far ahead in the long run by receiving a tax-free 7½ percent. Tennis became their sole recreational pursuit and he stopped playing tennis during the week days. More importantly, Bob went back to work. Bob's counselor slowly got him out of his entrepreneurial investments with his capital intact. The moral of the story at this point is quite simple: Bob got his life so complicated that he lost control over it, and all of these complications interfered with his productivity. Once his productivity had fallen off, everything else was jeopardized. One simply cannot do everything in life that one would like to do. Some decisions must be made and tradeoffs are crucial.

Ralph is in another situation, admittedly a rare one, for he is exceedingly rich. He had most of his money in the stock market and enjoyed managing it himself, but he also liked to travel and relax in some of the world's more plush retreats. It is difficult to manage your portfolio from the Riviera or Tahiti. As his other pursuits in life took more and more of his time he did less and less money watching. He was caught asleep in the bear market of the early 1970s and lost a good portion of his fortune. He quickly saw that he would not be able to pursue his desired style of life and adequately look after his money, so he placed the management of his portfolio in the hands of a person he had come to trust and whose judgment seemed sound. The counselor managed Ralph's money full time. Even in the bear market of 1973-1974 the advisor turned in an outstanding performance while Ralph continued his leisurely pursuits. Admittedly, Ralph was lucky. Other people have tried the same tactic and have been ruined when they chose the wrong financial manager. Substantial risks are always involved when you turn your affairs over to other people.

YOUR ASSETS OWN YOU—YOU DO NOT OWN YOUR ASSETS

Think about this for a minute: do you own your house or does your house own you? It is sitting there doing nothing while you have to work your tail off keeping it in good repair and paying its bills. The house commands a certain portion of your income and a certain part of your time. There is no escaping it. Every time you buy something—a boat, an airplane, a resort cabin—it is a claim on your time and attention. I once knew a man who had a rather large number of keys on his key ring. He would complain daily that each key was a worry, a responsibility, and claimed that he was trying to get rid of keys. That was just another way of saying that each asset is a worry, a responsibility. Each key represented a lock on one of his assets.

SIMPLIFY YOUR LIFE TO INCREASE PRODUCTIVITY

The moral should be clear to you by now. Every time you complicate your life it will take something out of you—something will have to give way and usually it is your productivity. Make a list right now of all the demands upon your time. Who and what demands your attention and time? Now go down that list and ask yourself some brutal questions about the necessity of each time expenditure. What can you do, what can you delete, that will give you more time for what you really want to do? Then learn to say no and mean no.

Boilerplate and Rhetoric

Did you ever see a government defense contract? It is an unbelievably long document that runs page after page in small type containing all sorts of clauses in which the government lawyers have tried to anticipate everything that might possibly happen including a flood on the moon. It is inconceivable that any mind would waste time on such "boilerplate," the legal term used to denote all the standard clauses stuck in such legal documents. Talk about a waste of productivity! It is bad enough to think of the manhours wasted in drafting the document, but think of the millions of manhours of indignity heaped upon all of the contractors who are forced to read such nonsense. When the final study determines what has happened to put the damper on the productivity of the American economy, I am confident that a great deal of the responsibility will be laid at the foot of the legal profession. Those rascals can waste more time, theirs and yours, over their boilerplate and verbosity and in the end you have nothing to show for it.

Words, words, and more words. Rhetoric inundates us. We sit and listen for hours upon end to speakers who say nothing of any consequence. Time and again I have turned on the television to hear a President's speech in which he was supposed to make some startling announcements, only to waste an hour or so listening to all the garbage. No more! All of the pundits will have the speech condensed and digested by the time the morning papers are at the front door. I regret this situation because I would very much prefer to have my information first hand, not filtered through the press, but the politicians cannot say something clearly and simply. They have to encase it in boilerplate. Thus the rhetoric flows.

Business is no different. How many times have you sat through a convention listening to the windbags saying the same things over every year since they have been president? Well, stop playing the game. Just climb off the bus. Whenever possible, do not go to such meetings. However, there are times when you must.

You Can't Avoid All Meetings

Admittedly, you must be present at some meetings or you will suffer calculated revenge by members of your hierarchy. Okay, so do it! Play the game. Go to their meetings and let them talk. Just take some other work there with you, sit in the back of the room, and get something useful done. I am never without a pad of paper and a pencil. The amount of work I can get done during those meetings is amazing. Learn to turn such affairs to your advantage.

PART 7

Summary

Classic Career Blunders

One way of summarizing this book is to review the classic career blunders that cause untold misery to those who commit them. Practically all of them have been mentioned elsewhere, but let us put them all together for your review.

NO CAREER

Heading the list of blunders is not having any career at all, just drifting from one thing to another, not perceiving that life is passing by while nothing is being put together. Surprisingly few people are really aware of their careers, let alone realize that they have considerable control over them. They do not perceive their careers as processes amenable to management, that planning and positive action can advantageously affect one's career.

JOB JUMPING

The young person is allowed a few mistakes early in his career; some job changes are allowable. While a certain amount of trial and error is necessary, still, after a number of job changes, the person is looked upon as a job jumper, a stigma that makes many potential employers wary of the individual. Certainly you are entitled to change jobs when you are clearly improving yourself. No one can fault you for that. We have previously discussed all the socially acceptable reasons for changing jobs, so there is no reason to review that here. But after a person jumps around from job to job, seldom spending long at any one, that no matter what or how forceful the reasons may have been, the suspicion arises that something is wrong with that person. Potential employers reason that since your longevity at other jobs has been brief, they have no reason to expect you to stay any longer with them. Changing jobs is a serious proposition, and many blunders occur when changes are made unwisely. In many cases a change of job signifies the end of one career and the beginning of another. Thus, one can hardly make progress if one must continually start from the beginning. In a well-managed career, each job change should move the person along his career path on schedule.

ACCEPTING A POORER JOB

Ed was a successful engineer with IBM whose progress and salary had been more than satisfactory, but he was chomping at the bit for all the usual reasons common to people who feel trapped in large organizations. He encountered a persuasive promoter who was starting a computer organization and was wooed into joining the new organization as vice-president of manufacturing operations. The move was a terrible blunder. The new company lasted six months; Ed was on the street looking for work at a most unfortunate time. While the risks involved in Ed's move are obvious to most people, some situations pose even greater dilemmas.

Let's examine Ron's problem. He was an excellent associate professor at California State University before receiving an offer from a more prestigious university in the area, but it was to be an assistant professor, not an associate or full. Ron accepted the offer; he had to take a demotion in rank even though the pay was slightly higher. Two years later he was unhappy because he had not been promoted in the new school although he richly deserved it for he had done far more than was expected of him.

Finally he quit to accept a position in business. Ron had thought he could easily accept a reduced status in exchange for being a member of a more prestitious group but found that he could not. He missed his previous status and involvement in policy-making decisions. One should think long and hard before accepting a lower status, even in a more prestigious firm, for it may be difficult to get that status back, but admittedly the choice is all a matter of what one really wants. Some people opt for prestige.

Another example from the academic world: a major state university was recruiting a particularly promising young assistant professor from another state university. While they were offering him a $1,000 increase in salary, the rank they were talking about was the same. The man was only being interviewed because of his friendship for the person who was recruiting him. He was not at all interested in moving from one school to another without an increase in rank. The last afternoon of the recruiting visit, a professor of accounting suddenly shouted to the department head who was trying to hire the man, "You can't expect this man to come here as an assistant professor! He's that already. Get real! If you can't offer him an associate professorship, he has no business coming here and you have no business asking him!"—exactly the thought in the recruit's mind. This outburst shocked the hiring department head into increasing the offer to an associate professorship and he got his man. Hold out for a better position than the one you have. It makes little sense to move sideways or even worse, to move downward. That argument can be used effectively in negotiating.

DEAD-END JOB

Contrary to the adage that there are no dead-end jobs, only dead-end people, dead-end jobs do exist. Usually dead-end people stay in them, but the jobs nevertheless are there. If you remain long in a dead-end job, your career advancement comes to a screeching halt. Look around your company: you can see all sorts of positions that lead nowhere. Unless your career goal is the attainment of that position then you must view it as a passing phase in your career.

Norma, with an MBA from a Big-10 university in hand, sought a career in management with a large organization. She was quite talented, but unfortunately one of her talents was exceptional secretarial skills, a holdover from the position she held prior to entering the MBA program. She was a Katherine Gibbs protege. The president, who sought a good executive secretary for himself, had built a fire under the personnel manager, and her application caught his eye. Aha, Norma would fit the bill, so he sent her up to see the president and they got along famously. The president painted the job as a stepping stone into management so Norma accepted it. After a few months she realized that she was only a secretary, admittedly a highly paid and responsible one, but still a secretary. She was not in management; she was going nowhere. She was as high as she could go without gaining the management experience she needed. But her pay was so high, and the prestige and ego satisfaction so great, that she could not bring herself to leave her perch in the executive suite. She accepted her fate, but not without some regret. Norma still harbored the hope that somehow she might be able to move into operations. She was working from within, volunteering to do projects that would thrust her into the operational aspects of the enterprise.

TOO NARROW EXPERIENCE

Sitting before me was an engineer whose career was in the dust. He was forty years old and out of work. He had been laid off in the aerospace cutback of 1970. For the previous twenty years he had been employed as some sort of exotic valve designer, but it was much narrower than that. I didn't understand exactly what he did and evidently from what he said, no one else did either. No one else needed his skills, they were unique with his former company. He had spent twenty years narrowing himself to the point of being unemployable. He was back in school to get an MBA degree and start over again.

It is amazing how many people one meets whose skills are so narrow that they do not have much to sell. You meet them at cocktail parties: they can only talk about one thing. I remember well an offensive line coach who was a fine fellow, but a bit narrow. The only thing he knew was how to block. He could talk all night on different blocking tactics, but that was it. He could not ever talk intelligently about the game of football, but he did know blocking. His career has not amounted to much.

TOO VALUABLE EXPERIENCE

Think before you allow yourself to become indispensable at some menial position. Many jobs are extremely important and require a high level of skill, but nevertheless hold no position of power nor are they particularly well paid. Perhaps a traffic manager would be an example. A good traffic manager who can save a firm much money is a rarity. When management sees an exceptional person in such a position the temptation is strong to do everything possible to encourage that person to stay in that job. If you are not content to do so, then you must take actions to counter that tactic. The classic counterattack, of course, is to have someone on hand who can replace you. As we have seen, however, that also has its dangers.

Your Career

A ready replacement weakens your bargaining power in some respects and can pose some risks to you, depending upon how good you are and how good your subordinate is. These matters cannot be resolved in print, for they depend on the situation. However, be advised that you can become too valuable in a job.

CHARACTER ERROR

It does not take much to remember the newspaper headlines about all the careers that were shattered because of Watergate. Those people will never be the same for their sterling careers are tarnished beyond redemption. Presently alleged scandals in the Bell Telephone System threaten careers of many of their executives in Texas. The case is now before the court and at this point no one is quite sure of what happened. However, it is likely that some additional careers will be ruined. One man has already committed suicide because of whatever occurred. It is foolish to gamble your whole life on some short-term gains provided by cheating, lying, or stealing. Your character is one thing that you will need in all future jobs. Don't lose it!

MIDDLE-AGED FOOLISHNESS

Some men seem to get restless in their forties. Perhaps they have not had the success they think is due them or perhaps they are bored with whatever success they have had. Perhaps their family life has soured. There can be any number of reasons, but suddenly many middle-aged men do all sorts of damn fool things—running off with young women, throwing away successful careers, what-

---

ever. Perhaps the most extreme case I have encountered involved Carl, president of a sizeable subsidiary of a very large company. Carl was regarded as a very bright guy and a comer with a bright future in the industry. Somehow he got started blowing pot and graduated to bigger stuff. Soon he was into everything. He hired a bunch of young hippies in the office, so you can imagine how much work was getting out. Literally, according to the testimony of one of the vice-presidents, the place reeked so of marijuana that he had to get out of there. Since the vice-president was the only straight person in the office, he resigned when he saw no good would come of the situation. As is true in most cases sooner or later, the president was busted and had to resign from his job. His wife divorced him. He picked up a new lifestyle in the wilds of the western woods with some of his newfound acquaintances. His acquaintances allege that he is supporting himself by dealing in dope. If that is the case, he is headed for jail—a matter of time. Carl's bright career was totally destroyed by a combination of middle-aged foolishness and character flaws.

Middle age is a tough transition. Perhaps the concept of middle age is the culprit. People may not visualize or conceive of themselves as middle-aged. You are young until you are too old to buy or sell that lie. Mentally there may not be a middle ground.

One of my colleagues, Dr. M. McGill, has been studying a widespread phenomenon that he calls *Mid-Life Crises*. It comes with a realization that you are getting old and you aren't going to go any higher or you are not going to reach your goals. He maintains that the key to escaping mid-life crises is to have outside interests. Individuals who have devoted their life and their total being to the job are particularly destroyed when the job seems to have failed to provide them with the success they sought.

LURED BY LOOT—THE MONEY PLAY

Money has been at the root of many career blunders when the person opts for some alternative solely on the basis of what it apparently pays. It has been said time and again to graduating students, "Do not pay much attention to beginning salaries, for they don't mean that much," and almost universally the students ignore the advice and choose the top-paying job. "A bird in hand is worth two in the bush," is heard many times over.

Jerry comes to mind as an example of this nonsense. When he graduated from the University of Oklahoma some twenty years ago, he took the highest paying position offered him, which was quite good because Jerry was an attractive prospect as a super salesman. He went with a small firm selling chemicals to the construction industry and did rather well. Another firm saw his performance and lured him away by offering him more money. Thereafter followed a series of jobs, each more attractive than the previous one from the standpoint of money. Twenty years down the road, Jerry found himself doing things he no longer liked doing. He was still selling and making money at it, but he did not like the company that employed him, he did not like the product he was selling, and he did not like his customers. Money had led him where he was. Moreover, he was at the age when sales reps tire of the daily battle and want off the road to get into management. Well, Jerry should have thought about that sometime previously for he had not obtained any experience qualifying him for management. He was a sales rep and was going to be for the rest of his life. He was lured by money into situations that did not hold what he really wanted.

PLAYING IN THE WRONG LEAGUE

If you want to be successful, then you had better find out what league to play in and stay there. Phil had some modest success in the investment business in Salt Lake City, but his wife and family were not happy there; they wanted to move to Southern California. They had fallen in love with Newport Beach, so they moved there and Phil opened an office that put him out of his league. The market in Newport Beach was tremendously more complex than the one Phil had been used to. He was a fish out of water. He did not have the social contacts. While he had primarily depended upon selling mutual fund shares in Salt Lake City, the Newport Beach residents were not particularly interested in them. His type of operation was not the way the new market wanted to do business. He lasted six months and then, with savings exhausted, left town. When you find a place where you are a winner, you had better give long thought before leaving that place.

ENVIRONMENT

Environment is a perplexing problem, because most of us would like to live in surroundings that particularly suit us. Unfortunately, we usually cannot make as good a living there as we can in less enticing places. People who are wedded to one place may pay a price for it in their careers. I saw this in two different areas. Time and again in Colorado I would meet people who would not leave that state, although offered much more attractive jobs elsewhere. They would remain in their jobs just to stay in the

Boulder-Denver area. Nothing at all is wrong with these value judgments; in fact, perhaps these people are wise in putting their environment ahead of money and power. But this is a book on careers, not on personal happiness, so let us keep those matters separate. Success and happiness are not necessarily the same.

In Southern California the same phenomenon is continually witnessed. During the unemployment surge of the early 1970s many engineers could have obtained employment in Texas but refused, preferring to stay in Southern California. I will not repeat some of the utterances these people made about their preference for starving in Southern California over going to Texas for I now live in Texas and am allergic to rope.

HOMETOWN

Again we have a debatable point. Without a doubt many careers have prospered in hometowns where good use was made of existing contacts. Similarly, other careers have been stifled by the hometown crowd for these people would have advanced faster elsewhere.

Another career blunder involves the person who goes home after spending a period of time elsewhere. Philosophers from time immemorial have observed that "you can't go home." Of course, they are talking about something other than just physically returning to the place of one's childhood. The successful person's interests, intellect, and talents grow immensely as he matures and becomes a different person than the one who left home years previously. Thus when he goes home to renew old acquaintances, he finds the old rapport evaporates quickly as others perceive the changes in his personality.

Frances had a promising, brilliant career ahead of her because she was an able, bright, young woman in the academic world. For some reason, the lure of her hometown was so strong that she accepted a job as a professor at a small local institution. Her career was over; she had gone home to vegetate. Let us hope that her psychological satisfactions were sufficient to offset the loss of the career that was due her. An update to Frances' career: she threw in the towel shortly after the first edition was published and begged for her old job in Dallas and was accepted back into the fold. Since that time she has made two other career blunders. She took an administrative job at her school at which she was a dismal failure for she hasn't the temperament for administration. Upon that failure, she is now trying a staff position in industry. No one knows what she is trying to do.

FINANCIAL MISMANAGEMENT

Many careers fall apart because of the stresses placed upon them through the mismanagement of personal finances. Some people manage to get themselves into such financial hot water that it affects their work.

The case of Brad is a classic, a man whose identity must be carefully disguised because he held a prestigious position. Unfortunately, just prior to accepting that position he had been involved in a business deal to which a bank had loaned a great deal of money requiring the personal signatures of the principals in the venture. The enterprise failed because of the operating partner's inadequacies. As is typical, the bank went after the person on the note with the most money, and that was Brad. He could not declare bankruptcy, for it would have ruined his career. He had to pay up, so he made arrangements with the bank to pay off the money over time. His salary was such that they knew they would eventually get their money. However, the payments placed such great strain on his personal finances that it caused difficulty at home, ultimately resulting in divorce. Brad was technically insolvent and divorced, a terribly destructive emotional trauma for him. During the three years this situation was developing, Brad had to spend a great deal of time trying to resolve these matters, trying to work his way out of bankruptcy and trying to save his marriage. In spending so much time on personal affairs, he neglected his job. His employers became unhappy with him and fired him. Now he has nothing. Brad's inability to manage his personal life ruined his career.

One simply cannot do much of a job for his employer when harassed by personal problems. Moreover, highly competent people are prone to hold people who mismanage their affairs in contempt. They reason, "If the person cannot manage himself, why should we believe he can manage other people?"

ENTREPRENEURSHIP—OWN YOUR OWN BUSINESS

Deep down in the hearts of a lot of business bureaucrats lurks the secret desire to own a business. "I'd like to be my own boss for a change." Of course, this is a delusion, for few entrepreneurs report feeling that they are their own bosses. It seems to them as if everyone else is the boss, but that is another tale. Occasionally a bureaucrat makes the jump. Sometimes the enterprise works out; usually it does not.

Let me tell you about Dan, a vice-president of marketing for a large national concern, who was unhappy. He was being harassed by some superiors and subordinates whom he considered incompetent. He was getting little psychological satisfaction from his job, even though he was exceptionally well paid. He had long harbored a desire to go into business for himself and he had financial backers. Finally he became sufficiently fed up with his situation that he decided to start his own business. He had the product in hand with which to begin so he made the telephone calls to get the money and his backers responded on cue. Three years later, after much hard work and great personal sacrifice, he threw in the towel. It was not because of unwillingness to work hard for Dan was a hard worker. Perhaps that was his trouble: he worked too much and managed too little. More simply, Dan was not an entrepreneur. He did not have the entrepreneur's philosophy and behavioral styles. Dan was a bureaucrat, a good one, but he did not want to admit that.

The urge to be an entrepreneur, while admirable, is fraught with danger. Starting your own business is a high-risk proposition and certainly not one to be undertaken without tremendous thought and preparation. Entrepreneurs do not usually come from the ranks of bureaucracy. Typically, the true entrepreneur has been an entrepreneur all his life. He hustled something or other on the street corner when he was five years old. The bureaucrat is not used to that type of behavior.

In Conclusion

It is hoped that the reader is now well aware of many of the factors and forces that affect his career and appreciates their complexity and perverseness. At all times one needs to understand that certain decisions can ruin one's career; careers lie in the dust never to rise again due to some seemingly insignificant events. Thus, the avoidance of such career-busting mistakes must continually be on one's mind.

It is also hoped that the reader now has a better idea of all the things that can enhance one's career. Careers are manageable to a large degree although admittedly luck is a significant element in many cases. But one does have some control over luck: you can give it a chance to happen.

After reading an early draft of this manuscript, a student asked, "But what would you say is the major thing I should try to do?" After a few moments of condensing thought, my reply was, "First make up your mind what you want to do and where you want to go. Then prepare for it meticulously, become an expert, dive in, and work like hell, be productive." True, this is trite, age-old advice, but it is still the truth. Those who are wont to put it down are but endeavoring to escape success.

And may the bird of success build a nest at your house.

Bestor, Dorothy K. *Aside From Teaching English What in the World Can You Do?* Seattle, Washington: University of Washington Press, 1977.

Bolles, Richard N. *What Color is Your Parachute?* Berkeley, California: Ten Speed Press, 1979.

Bolles, Richard N. *What Color is Your Parachute?* Berkeley, California: Ten Speed Press, 1979.

Calbert, Robert, Jr. *Career Patterns of Liberal Arts Graduates.* Cranston, Rhode Island: The Carrol Press, 1975.

Cohen, Leonard. *Choosing to Work.* Reston, Va: Reston Publishing Co., 1979.

College Placement Annual. College Placement Annual, P.O. Box 2263, Bethlehem, Pa. 18001. ($5.00)

Denves, Celia. *Career Perspectives: Your Choice of Work.* Worthington, Ohio: Charles A. Jones Publishing Co., 1972.

Dictionary of Occupational Titles (4th Edition). U.S. Department of Labor, ed. Washington, DC: U.S. Government Printing Office, 1977.

Encyclopedia of Careers and Vocational Guidance. Vols. I and II (3rd Edition). William E. Hopke, ed. Chicago: G.G. Ferguson Publishing Co., 1975.

Figler, Howard E. *PATH: A Career Workbook for Liberal Arts Students.* Cranston, Rhode Island: The Carrol Press, 1975.

Fox, Marcia R., Ph.D. *Putting Your Degree to Work.* New York: W.W. Norton & Co., 1979.

Haldane, Bernard. *How to Make a Habit of Success.* New York: Warner Books, 1975.

BIBLIOGRAPHY

Haldane, Bernard. *Career Satisfaction & Success: A Guide to Job Freedom.* New York: AMACOM, 1978.

Hawkins, James E. *The Uncle Sam Connection.* Chicago: Follett Publishing Co., 1978.

Irish, Richard K. *Go Hire Yourself an Employer.* Garden City, New York: Anchor Press/Doubleday, 1978.

Jackson, Tom and Davidyne Mayles. *The Hidden Job Market.* New York: The New York Times Book Co., 1976.

Jackson, Tom. *28 Days to a Better Job.* New York: Hawthorn Books, Inc., 1977.

Lovejoy's Career and Vocational School Guide. Simon & Schuster, 630 Fifth Avenue, New York, 1978. ($7.50)

Medley, H. Anthony. *Sweaty Palms: The Neglected Art of Being Interviewed.* Boston: CBI Publishing Co., Inc., 1977.

Mitchell, Joyce S. *The Men's Career Book.* New York: Bantam Books, 1979.

Occupational Outlook Handbook. U.S. Dept. of Labor, ed. Washington, DC: U.S. Government Printing Office, 1978-79.

Over 2,000 Free Publications: Yours for the Asking. Frederick J. O'Hara (ed.) The New American Library, Inc., P.O. Box 999, Bergenfield, N.J. 07621, 1968. ($0.95)

Peterson, Clarence E. *Careers for College Graduates.* New York: Barnes & Noble, 1968.

Powell, C. Randall. *Career Planning and Placement Today.* Dubuque, Iowa: Kendall/Hunt Publishing Co., 1978.

Psychology of Careers. Harper & Row, 10 East 53rd St., New York 10022, 1957. ($5.75)

Shingleton, John and Robert Bao. *College to Career.* New York: McGraw-Hill, Inc. 1977.

Souerwine, Andrew H. *Career Strategies: Planning for Personal Achievement.* New York: AMACOM, 1978.

Sources of Career Information in Scientific Fields. Manufacturing Chemists' Association, 1825 Connecticut Avenue, N.W., Washington, D.C. 10009. (free)

Sources of Engineering Career Information. Engineering Manpower Commission of Engineers Joint Council, 345 E. 47th St., New York 10017. (free)

Sources of Occupational Information. Division of Guidance and Testing, State Dept. of Education, 751 Northwest Blvd., Columbus, Ohio 43212. ($1.00)

"Starter" File of Free Occupational Literature. Irving Eisen and Leonard H. Goodman, B'nai B'rith Vocational Service, 1640 Rhode Island Ave., N.W., Washington, D.C. 20036, 1970. ($1.25)

Teal, Everett. *The Occupational Thesaurus,* Vols. I and II. Bethlehem, Pa.: Lehigh University, 1973.

Thain, Richard H. *The Managers.* Bethlehem, Pa.: The College Placement Council, Inc., 1978.

Thompson, Melvin R. *Why Should I Hire You?* New York, New York: Jove Publications, Inc. (Harcourt Brace Jovanovich), 1975.

Vogelsang, Joan, Ph.D. *Find the Career That's Right for You.* New York: Hart Publishing Co., 1978.
